I0488258

Know The Mechanics: How To Correctly Draw A Vehicle

Learn How to Draw a Vehicle from Start to Finish

Vehicle Book

By : Gala Publication

2

Published By :

Gala Publication

© Copyright 2015 – Gala Publication

ISBN-13: **978-1522721628**
ISBN-10: **1522721622**

Table of Contents

AIRPLANE

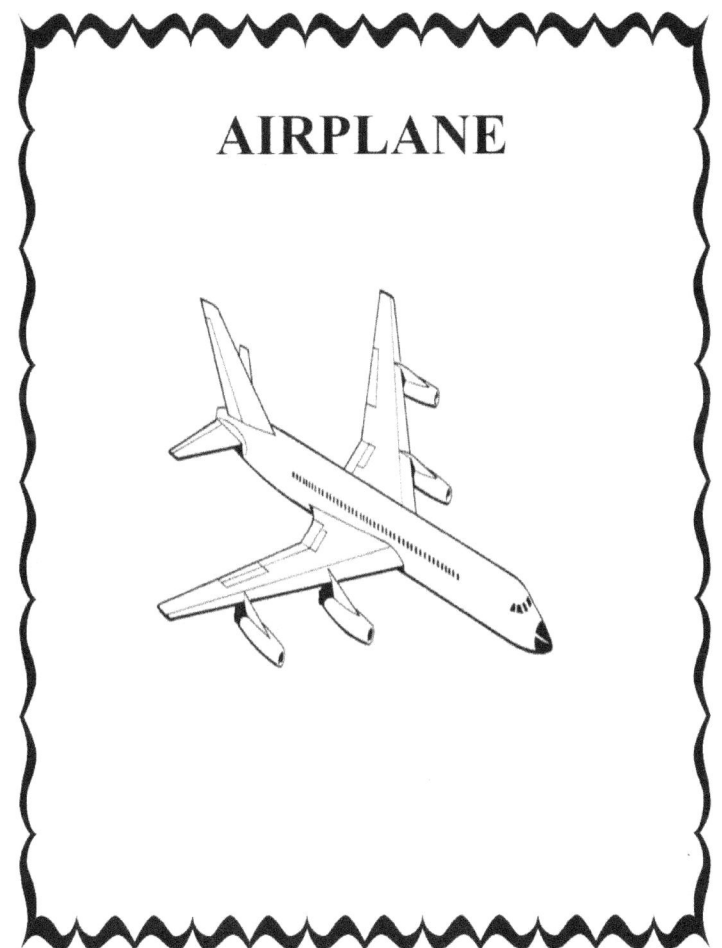

STEP 1

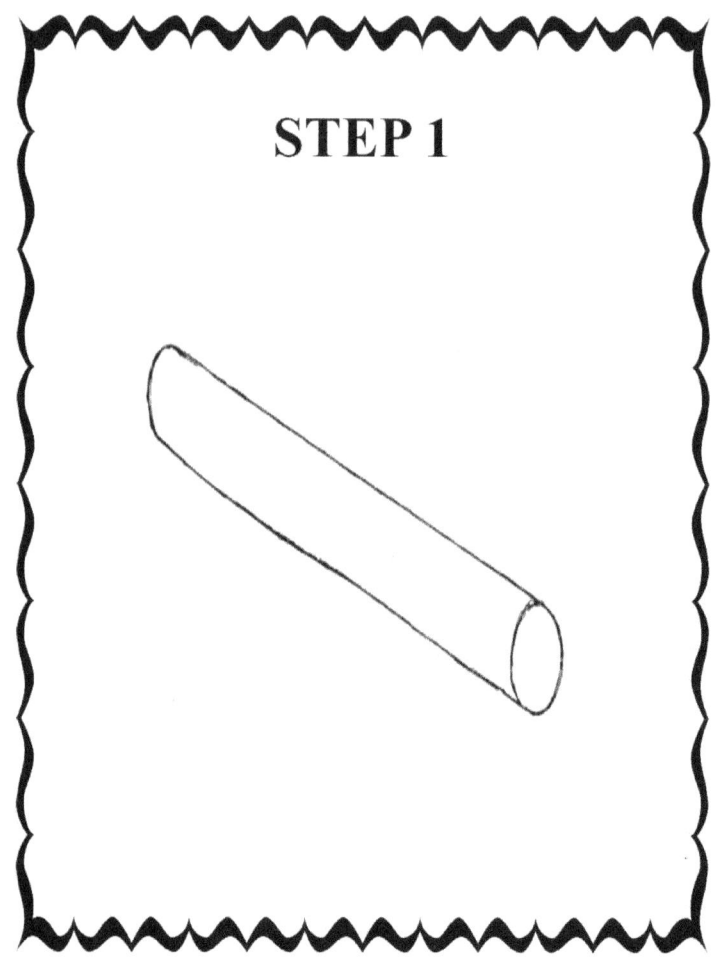

STEP 2

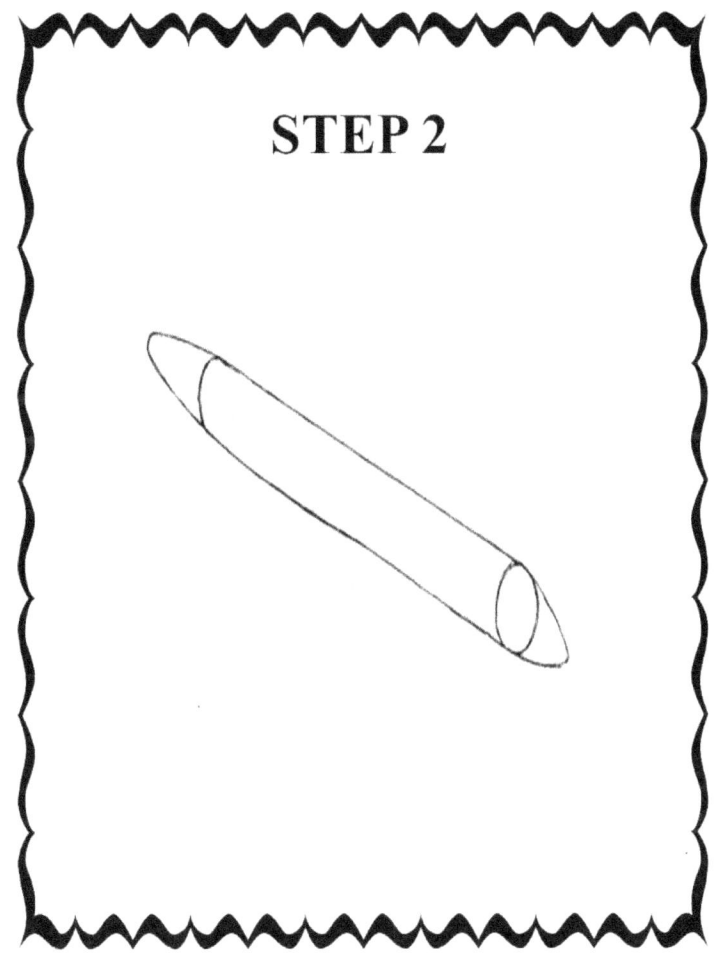

STEP 3

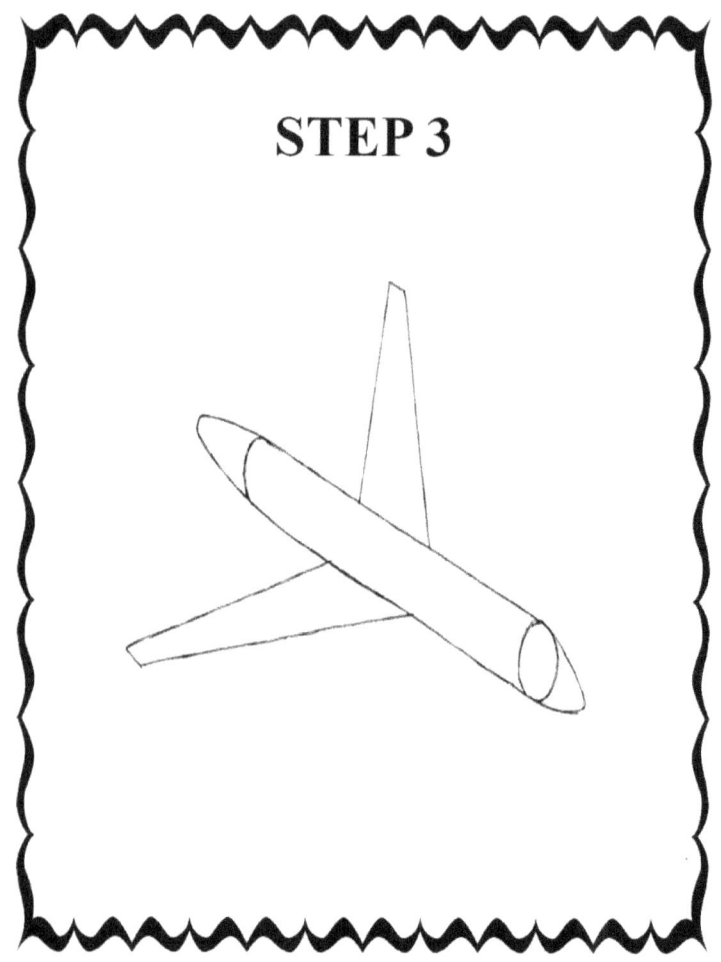

STEP 4

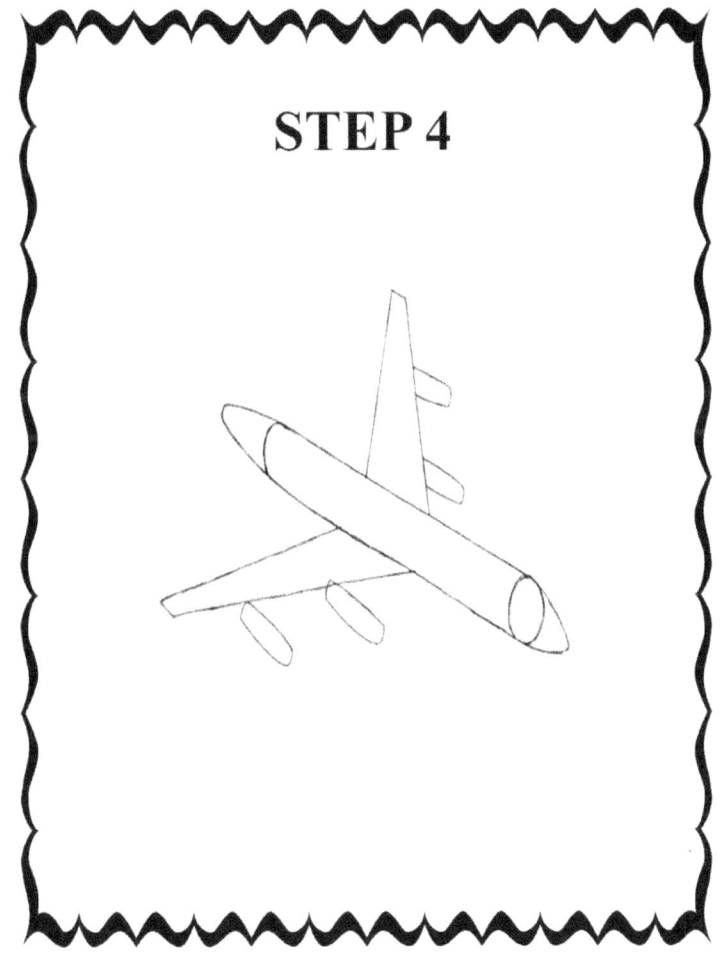

STEP 5

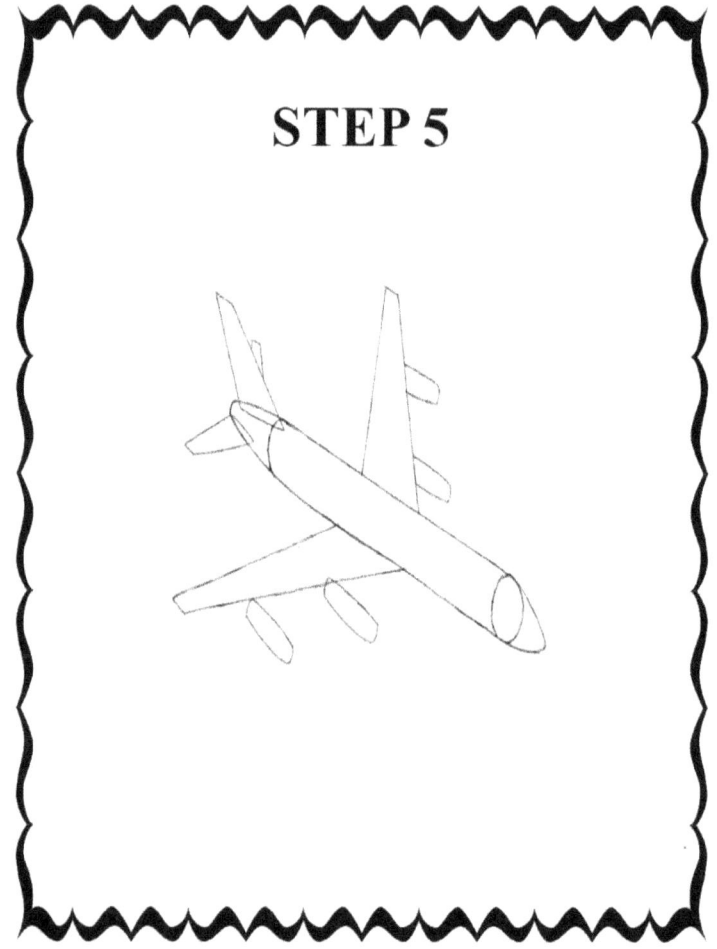

STEP 6

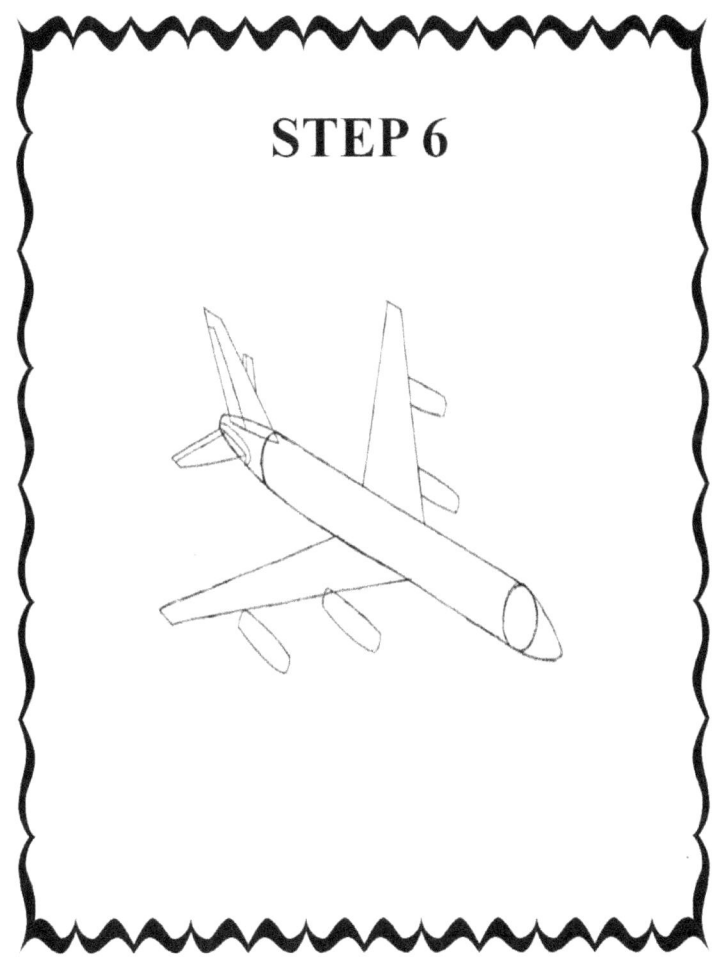

STEP 7

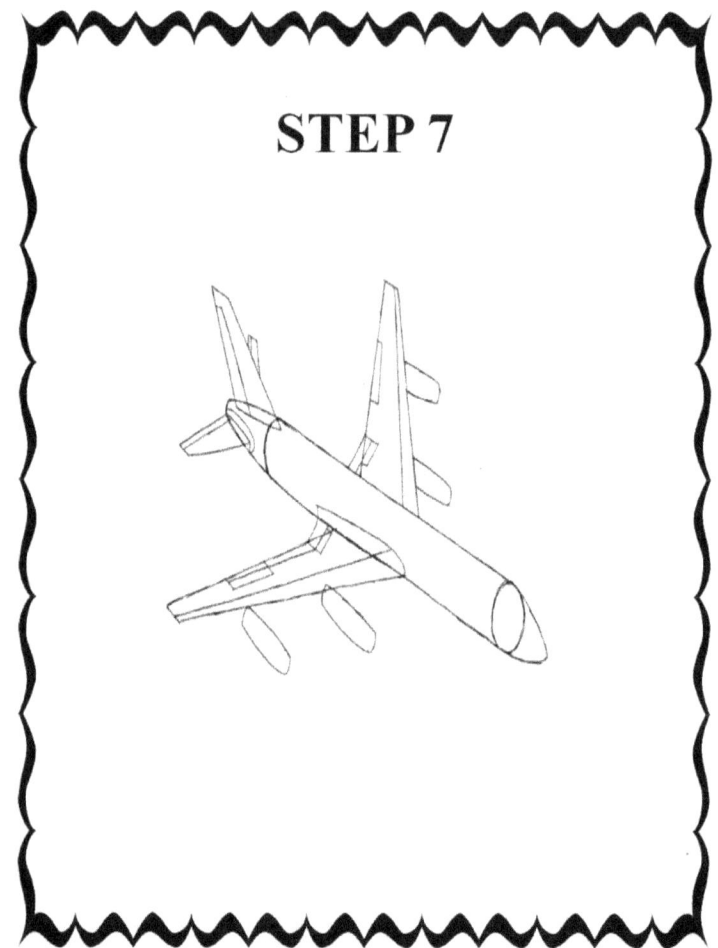

STEP 8

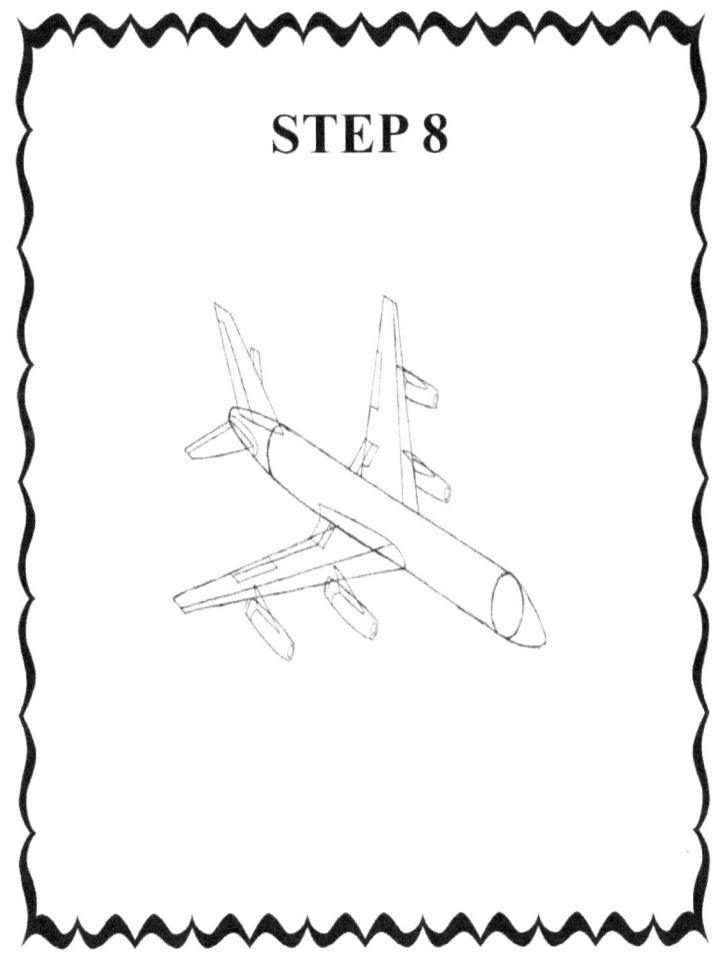

STEP 9

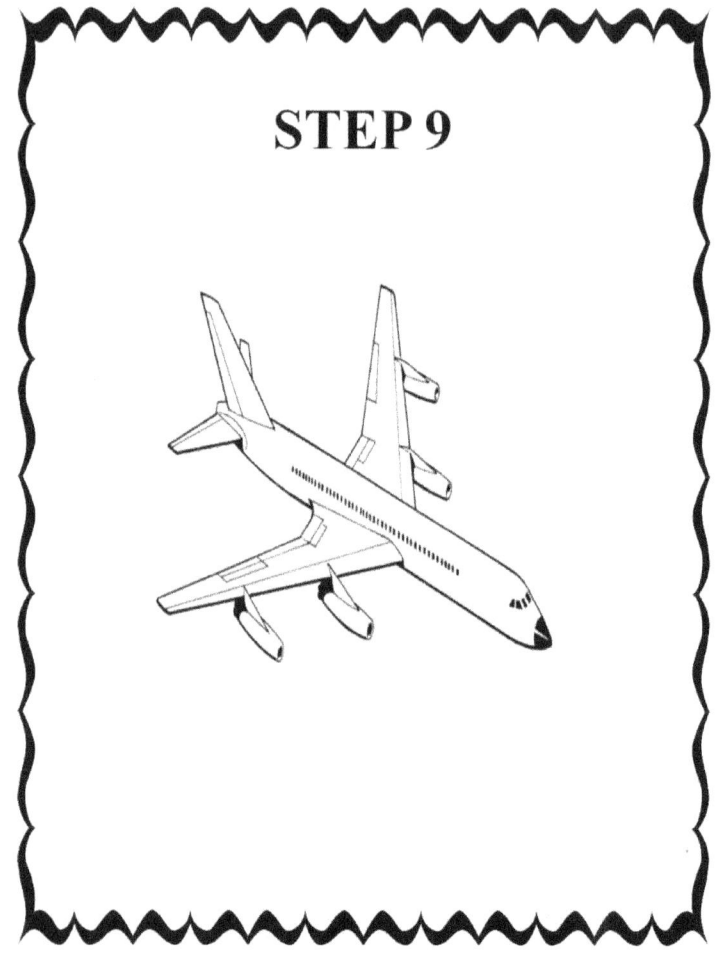

AMBULANCE

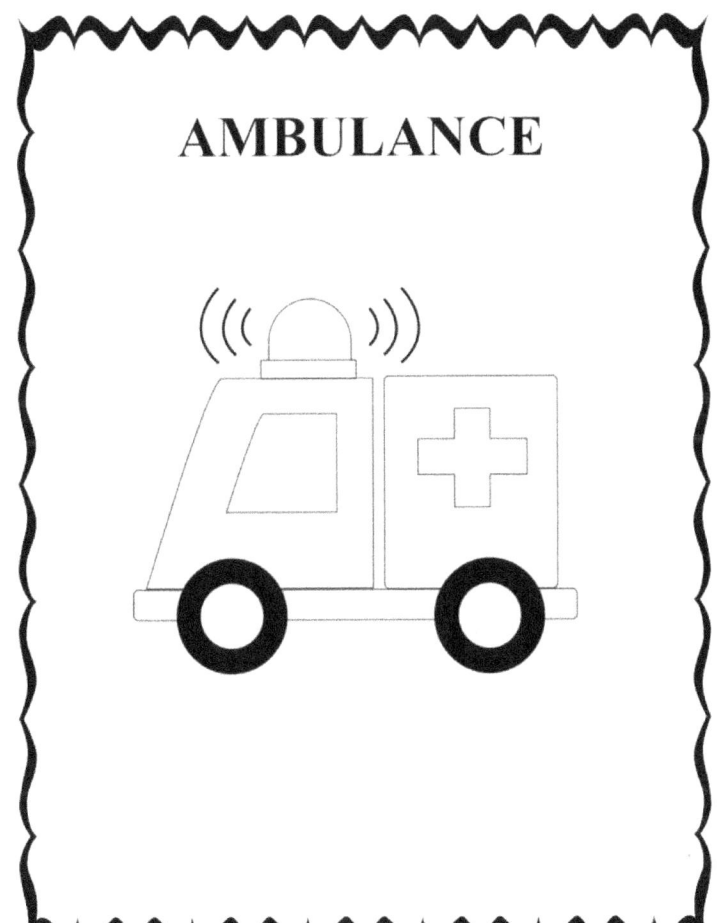

STEP 1

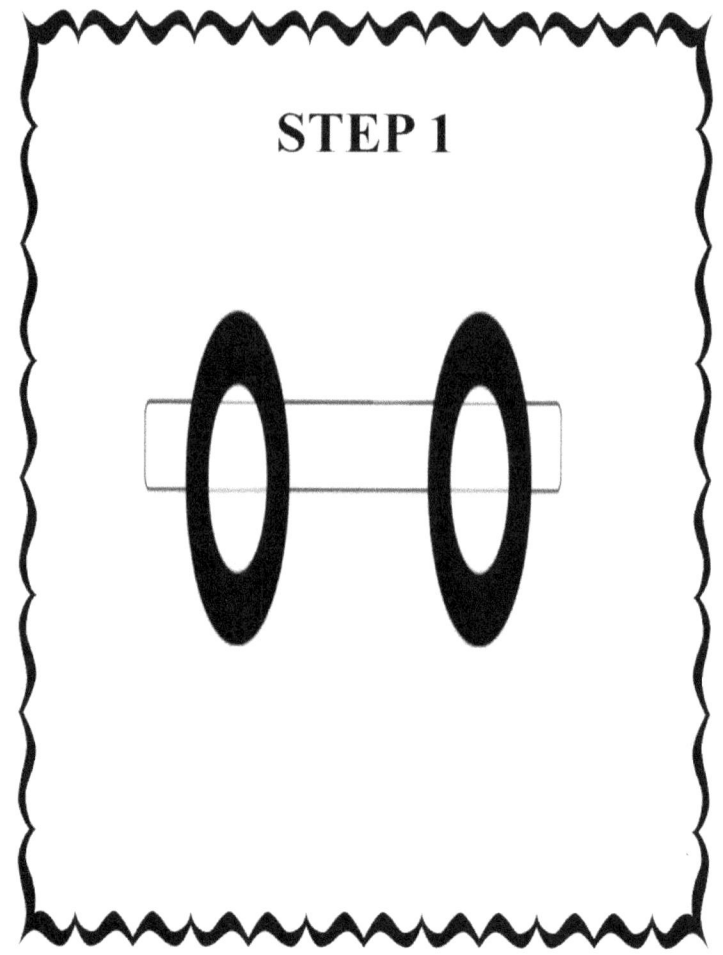

STEP 2

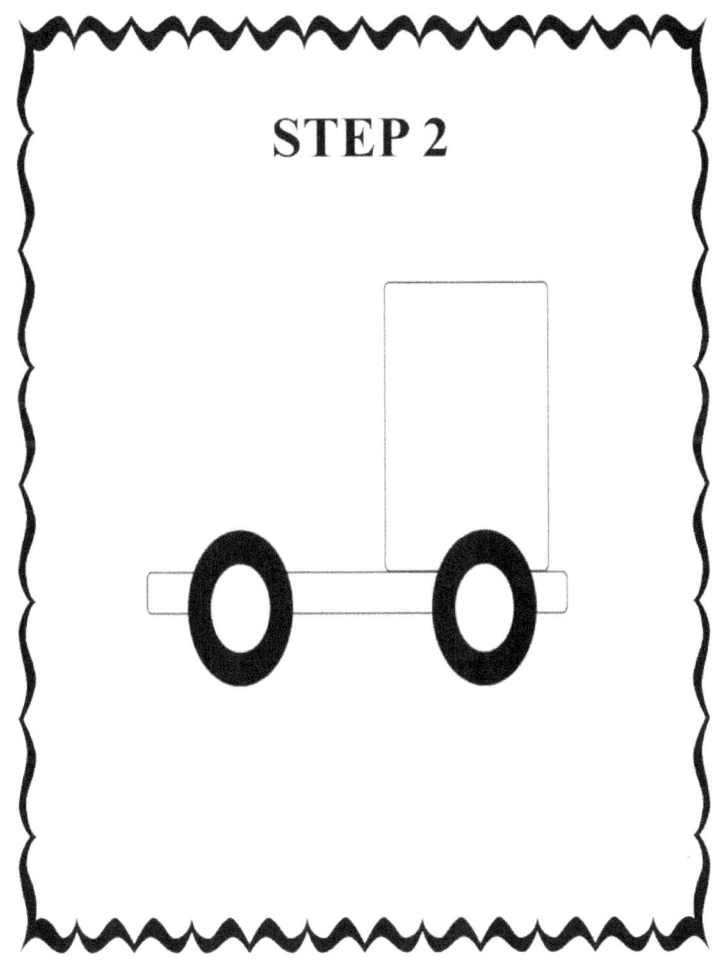

18

STEP 3

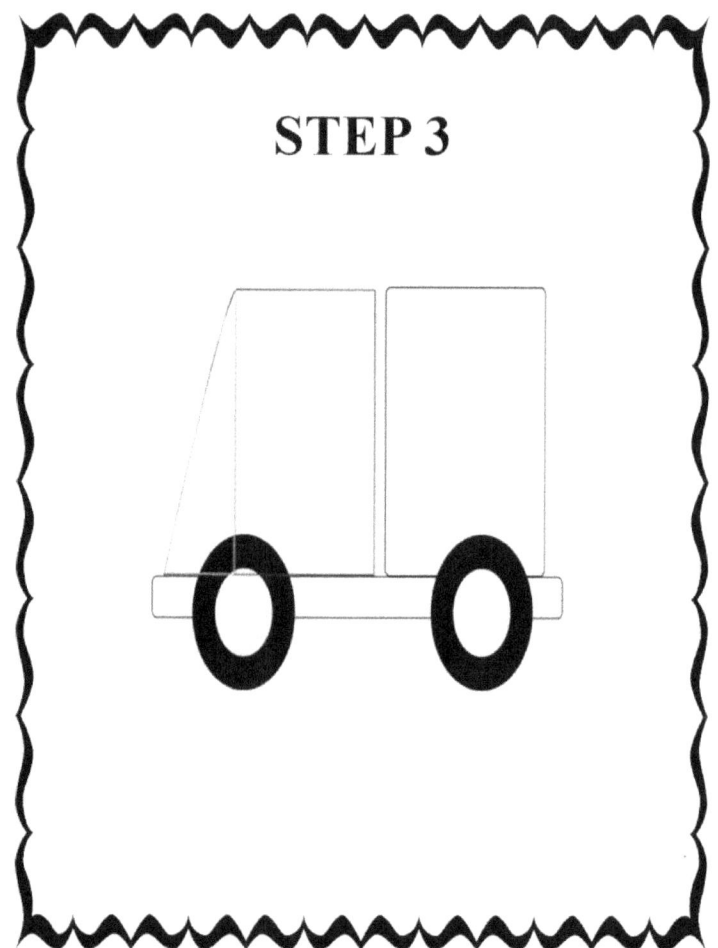

STEP 4

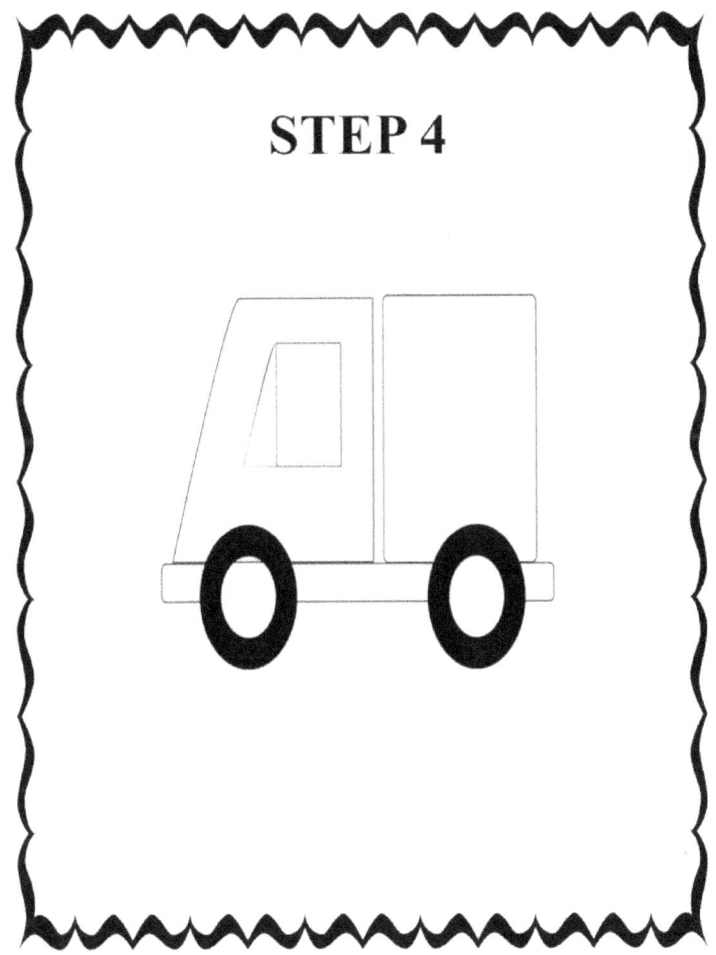

STEP 5

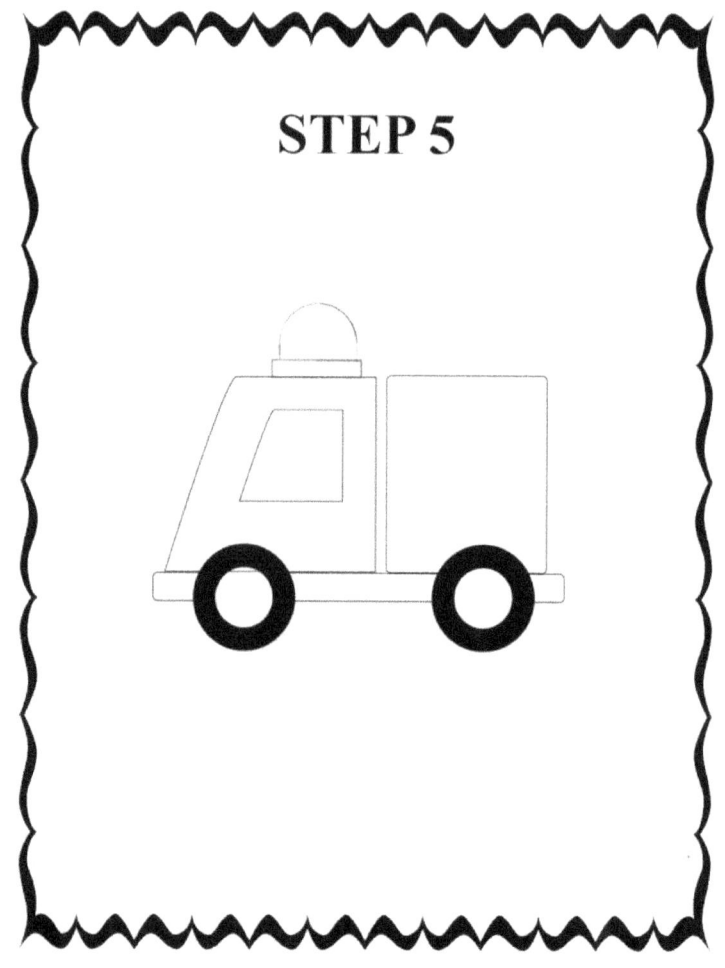

STEP 6

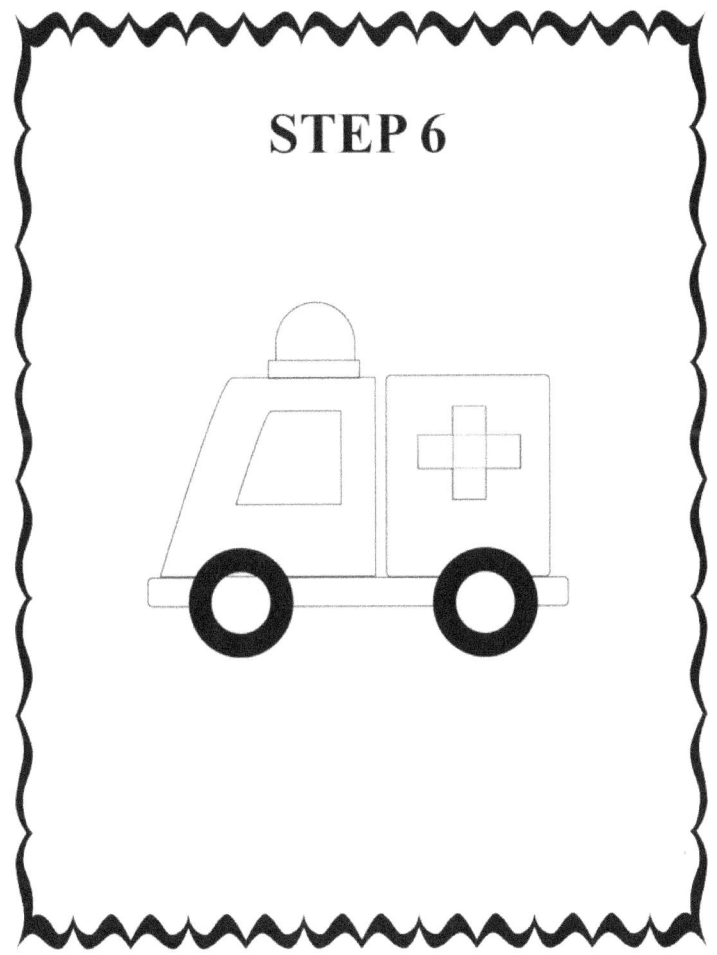

STEP 7

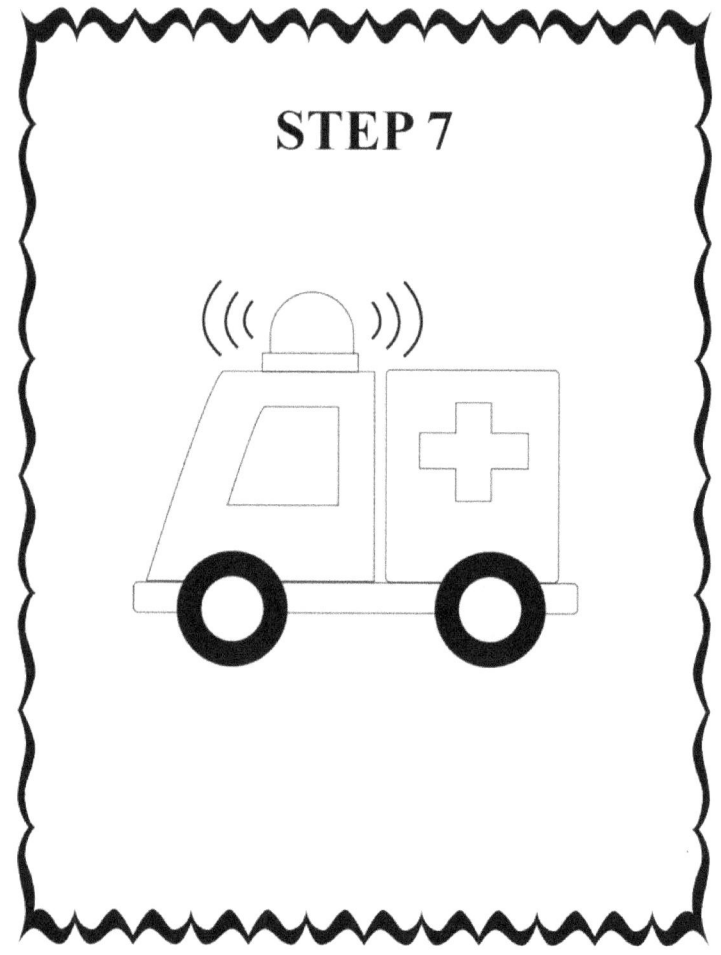

BICYCLE

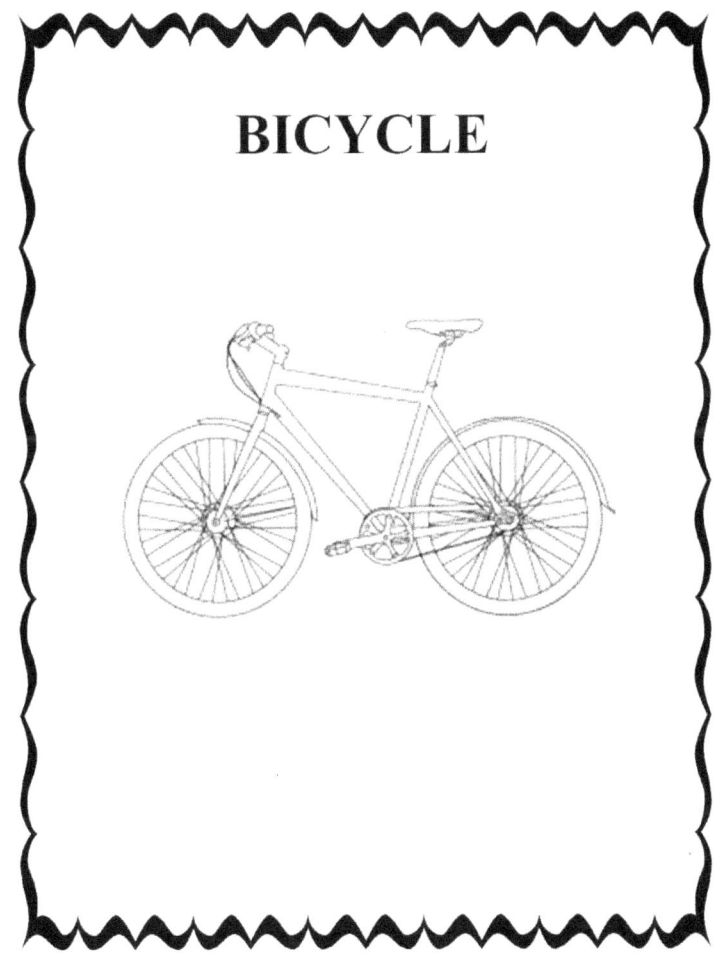

STEP 1

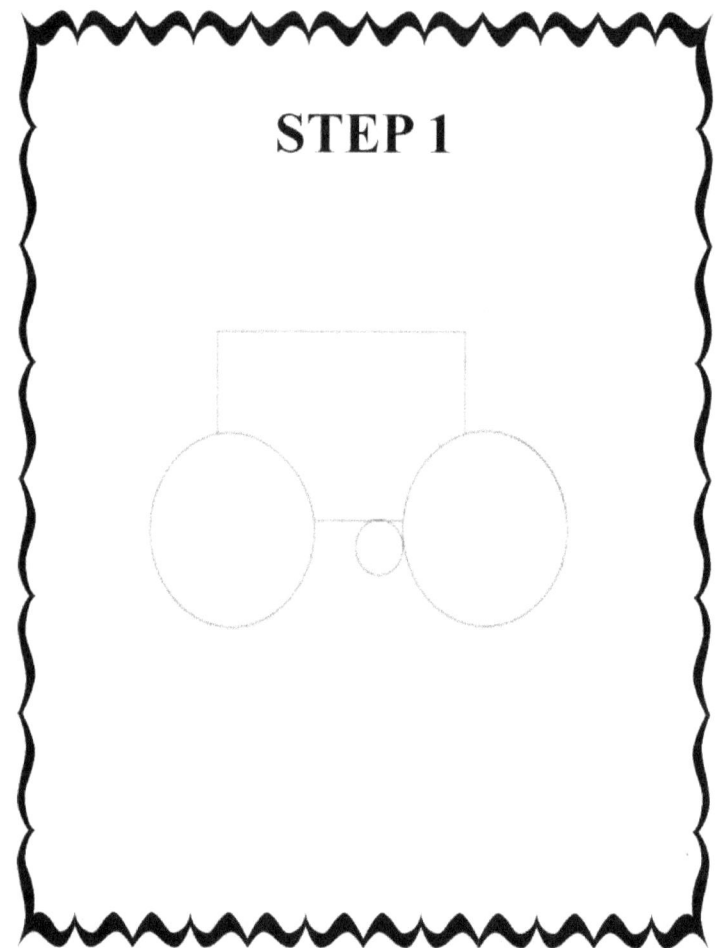

STEP 2

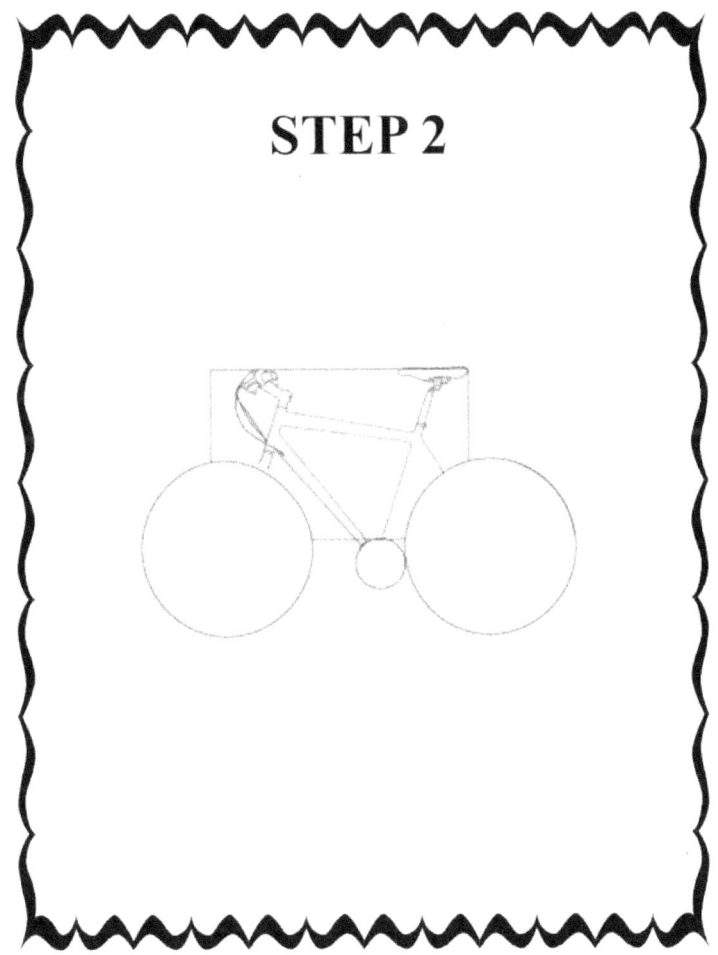

STEP 3

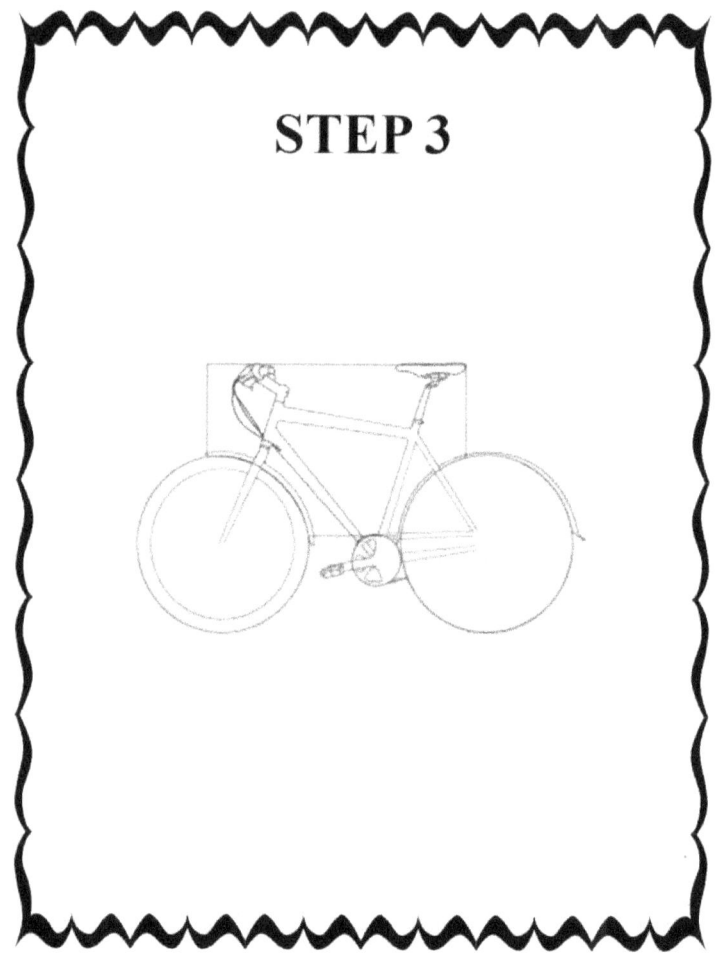

STEP 4

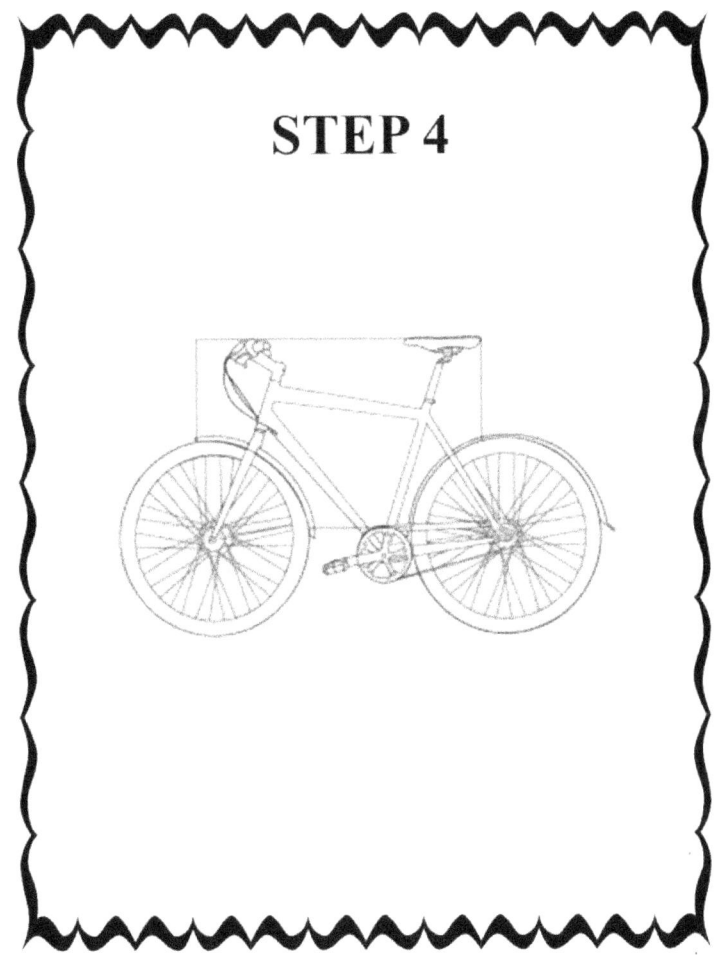

STEP 5

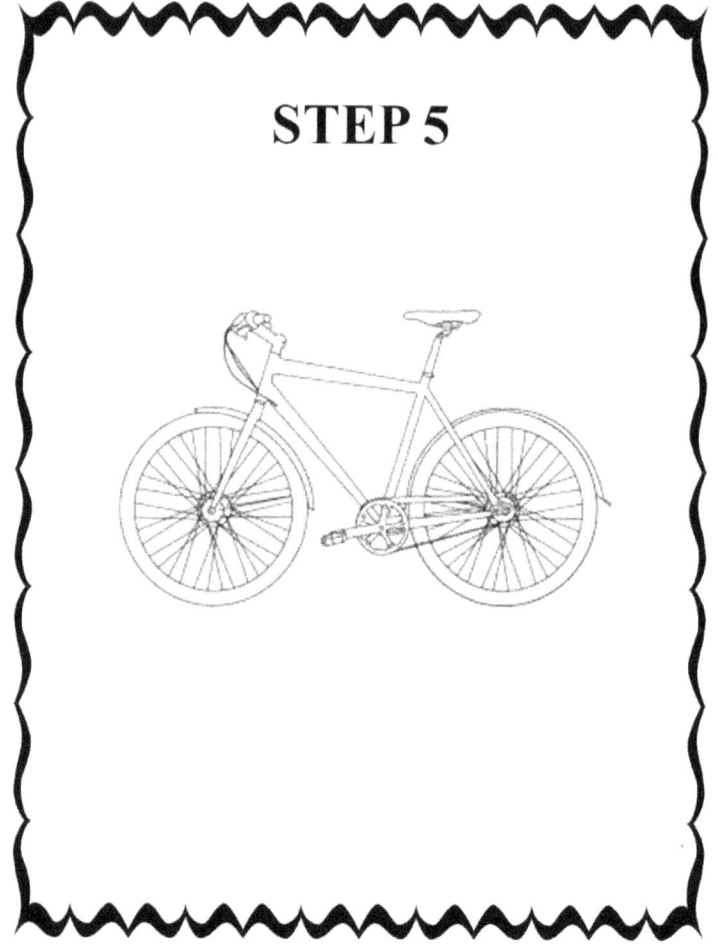

HELICOPTER

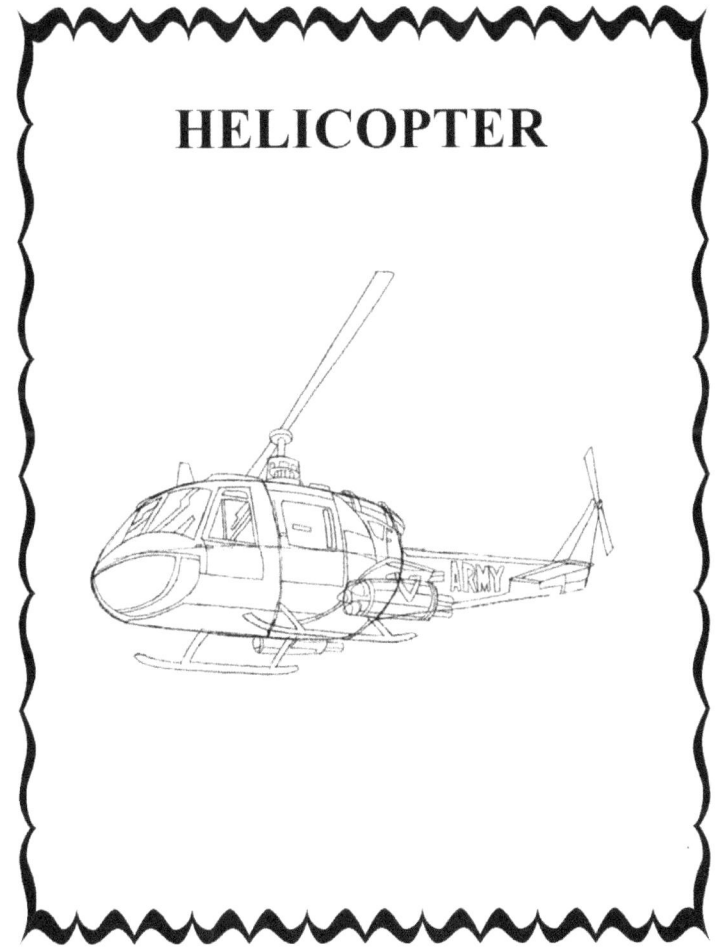

STEP 1

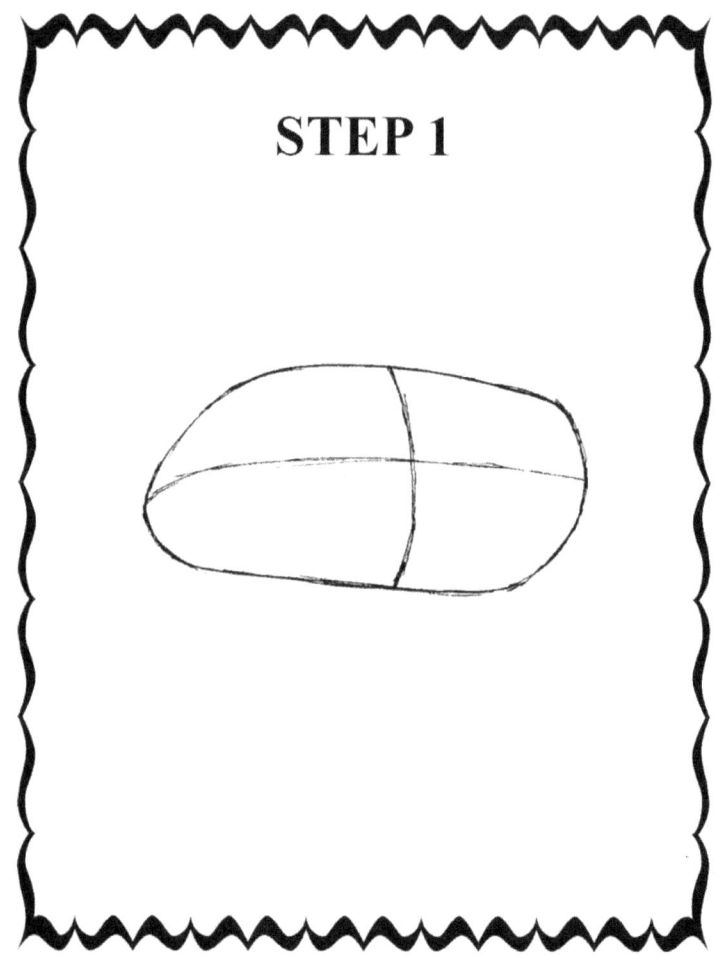

STEP 2

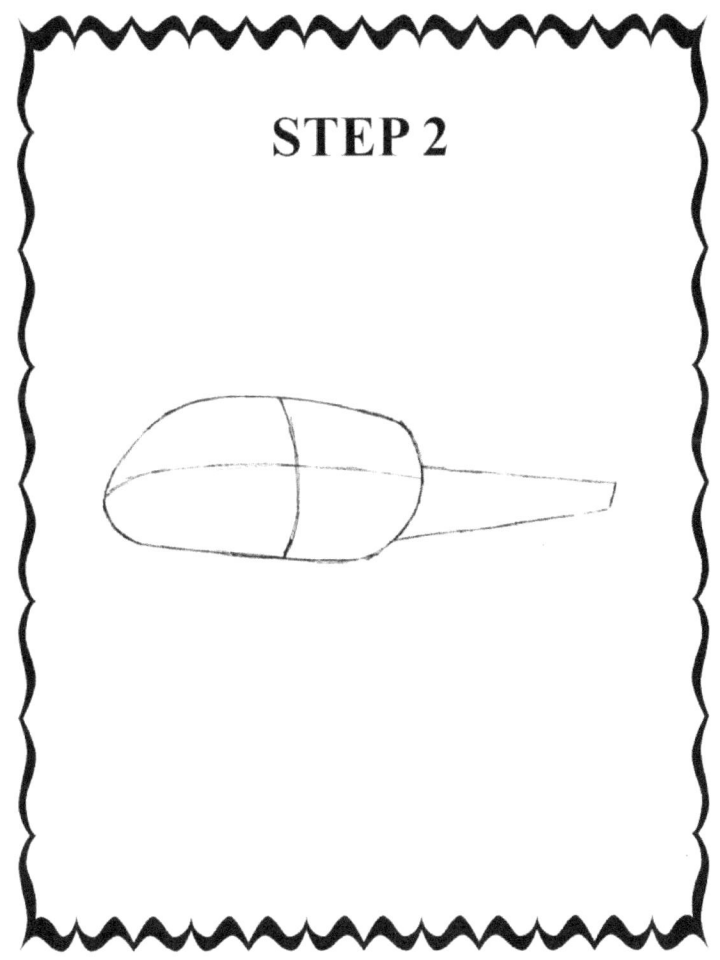

STEP 3

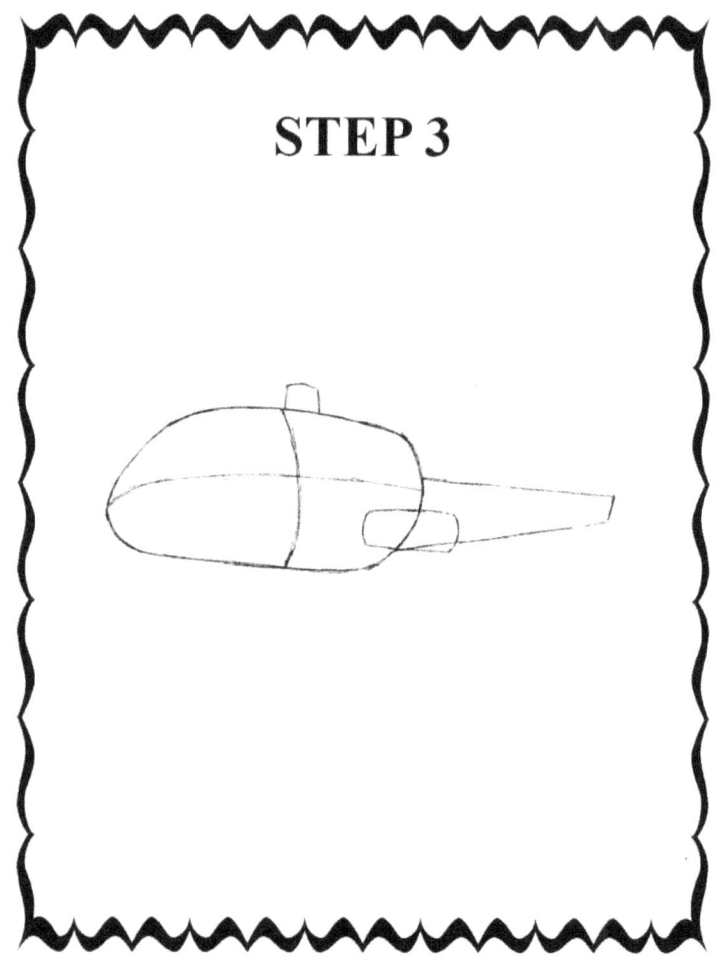

STEP 4

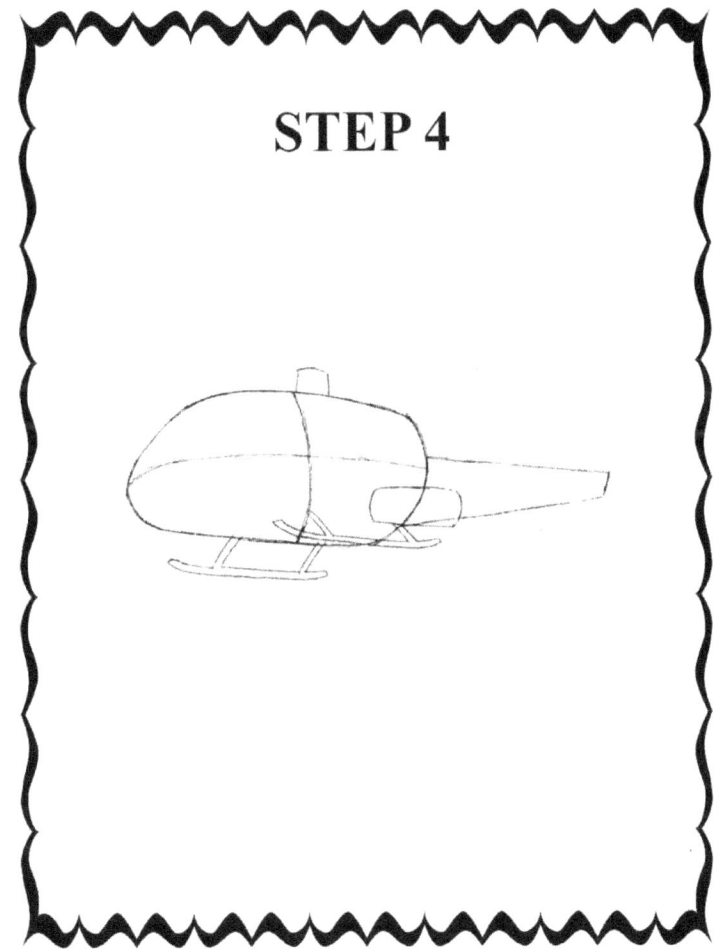

STEP 5

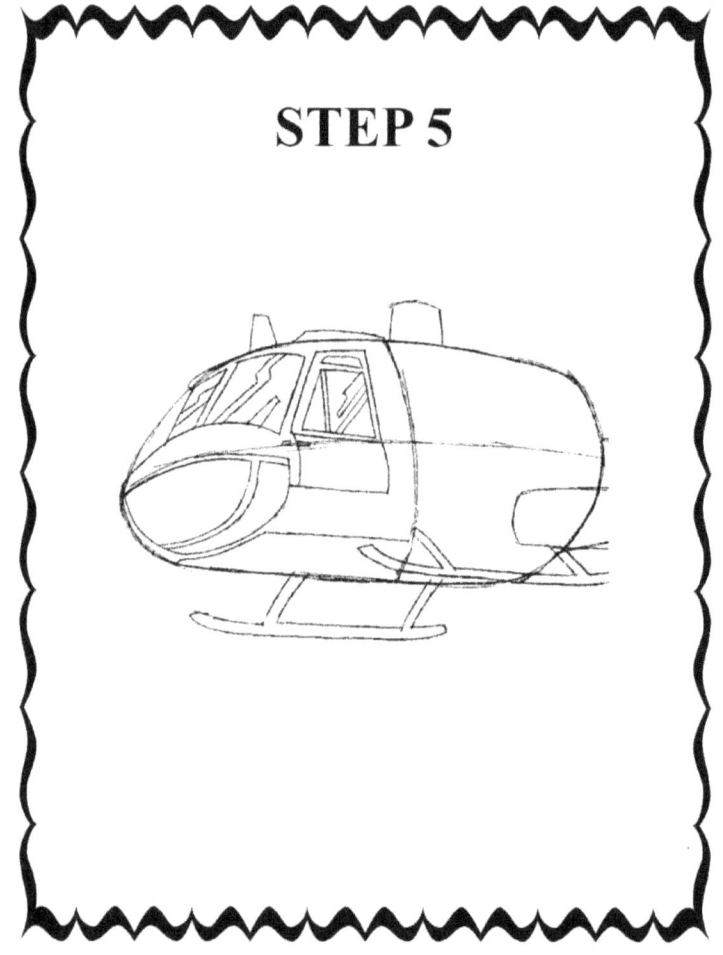

STEP 6

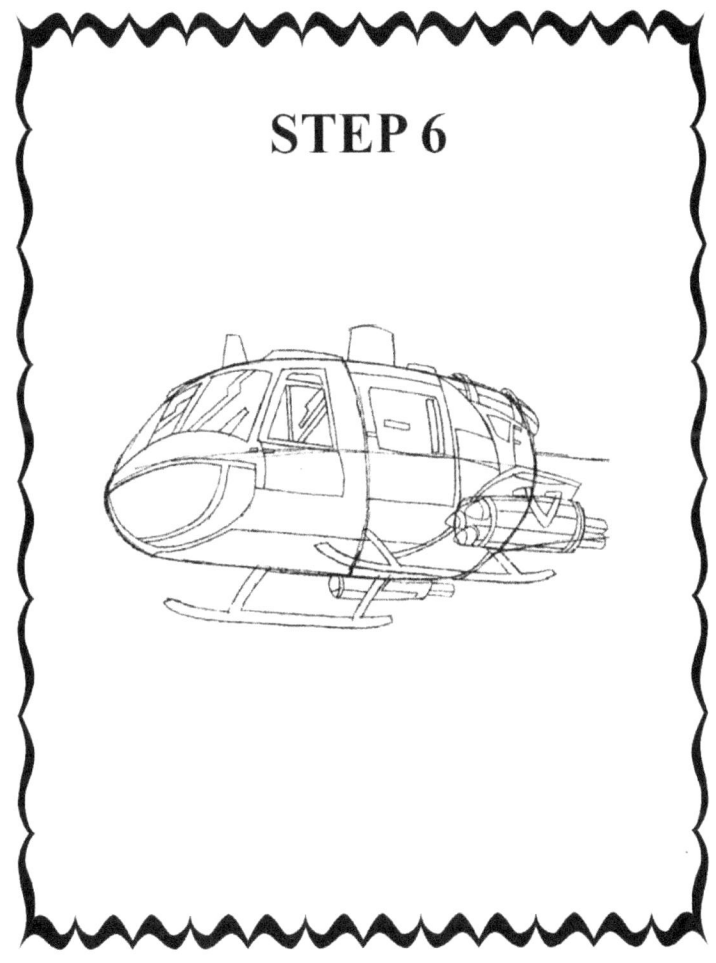

STEP 7

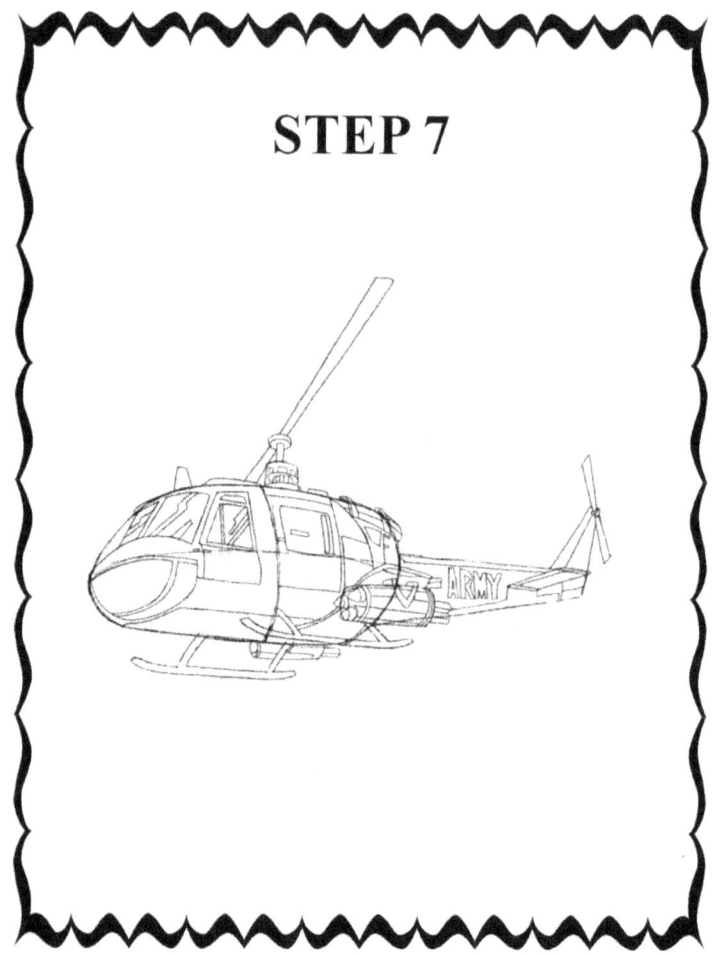

MOTORBIKE

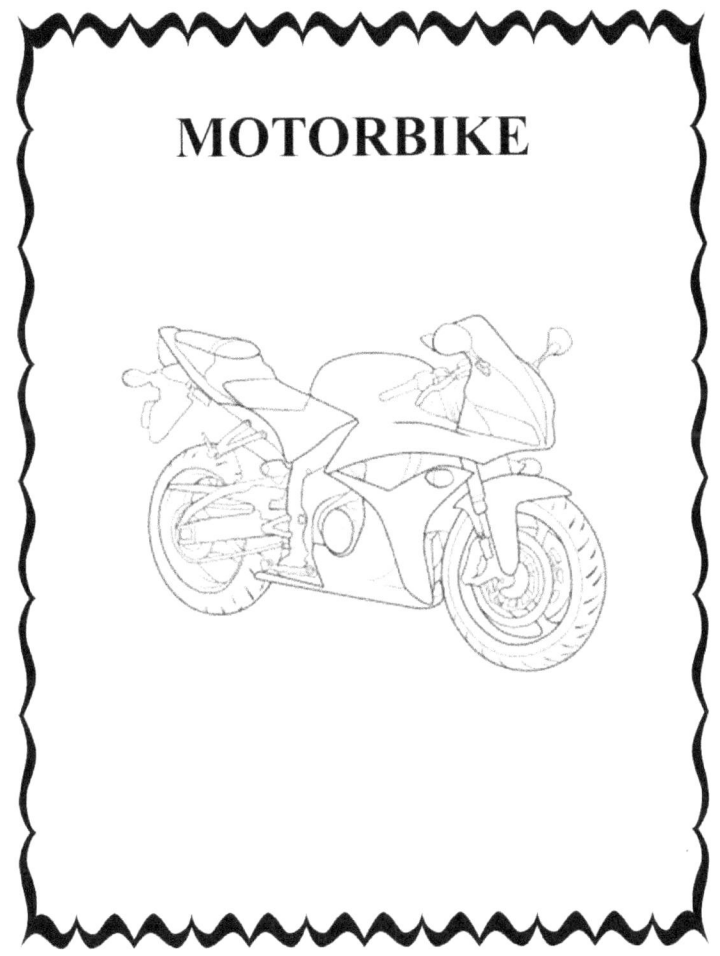

STEP 1

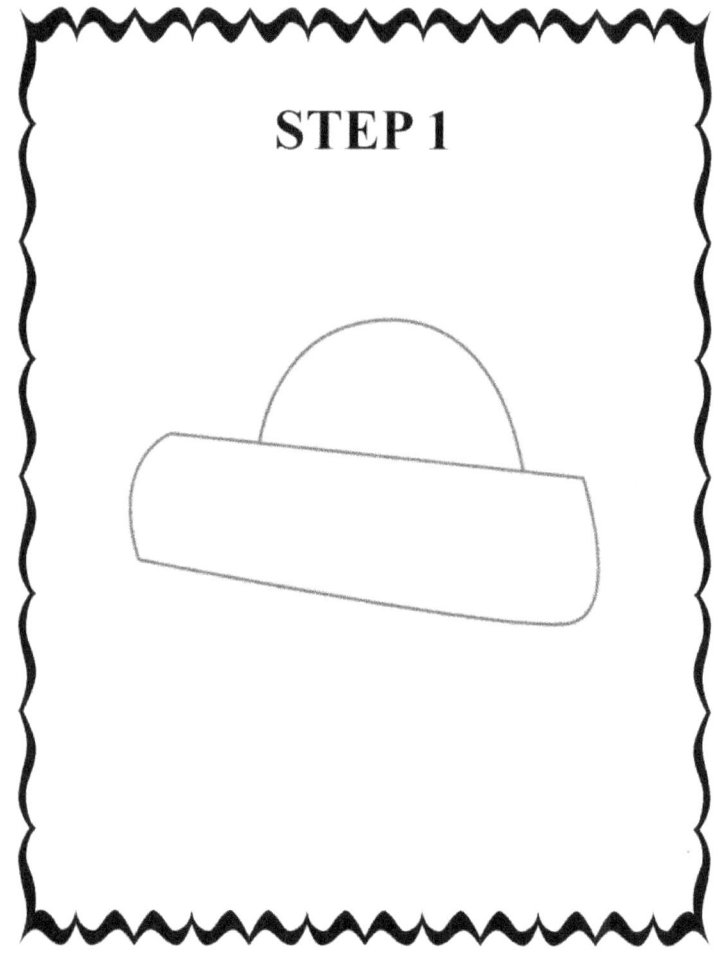

STEP 2

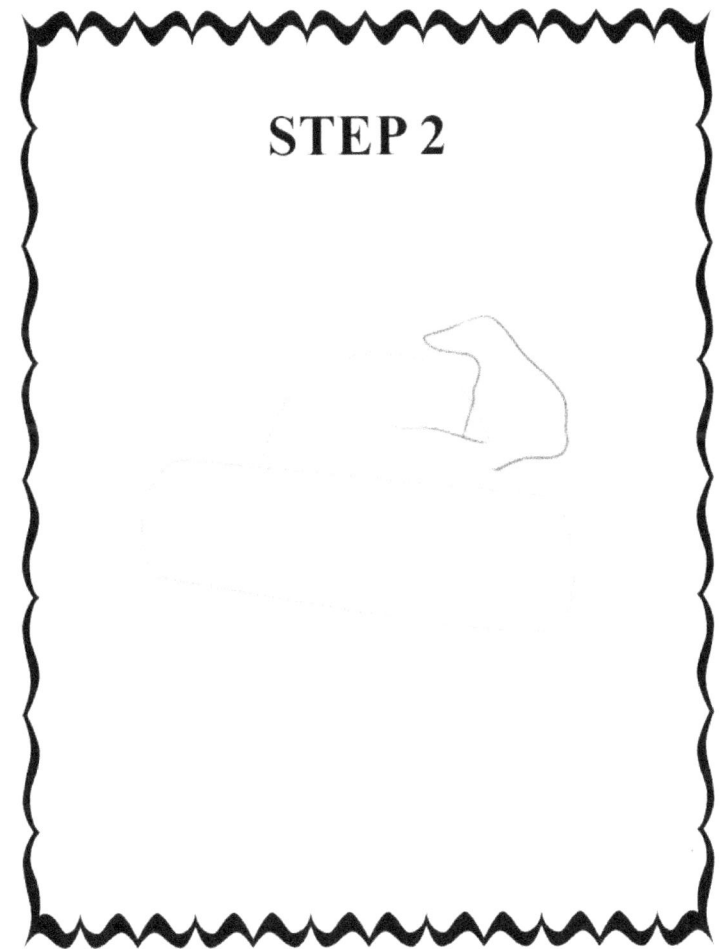

STEP 3

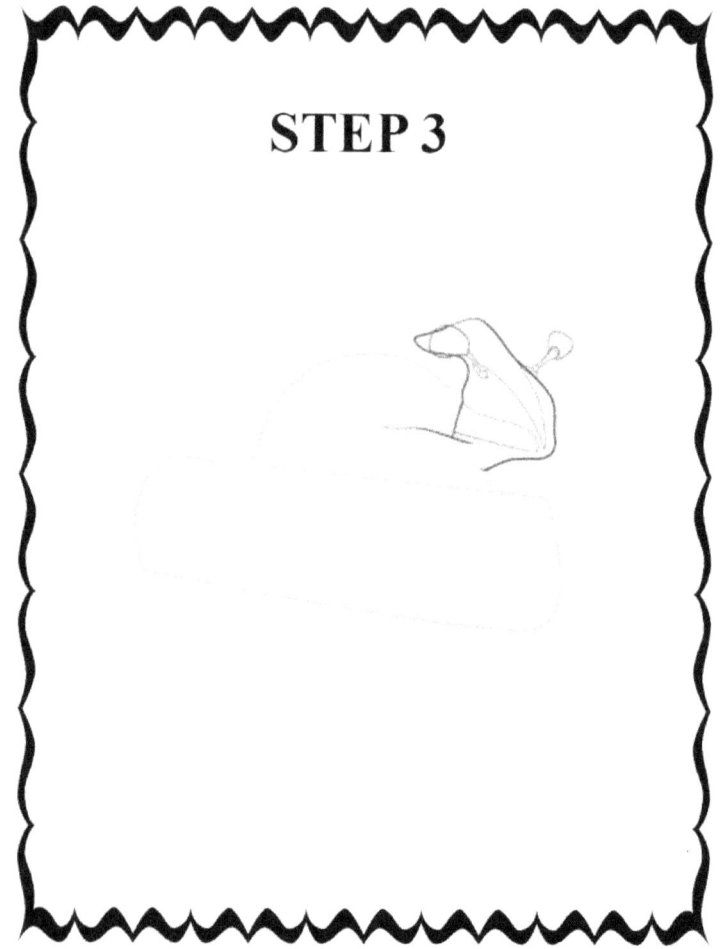

STEP 4

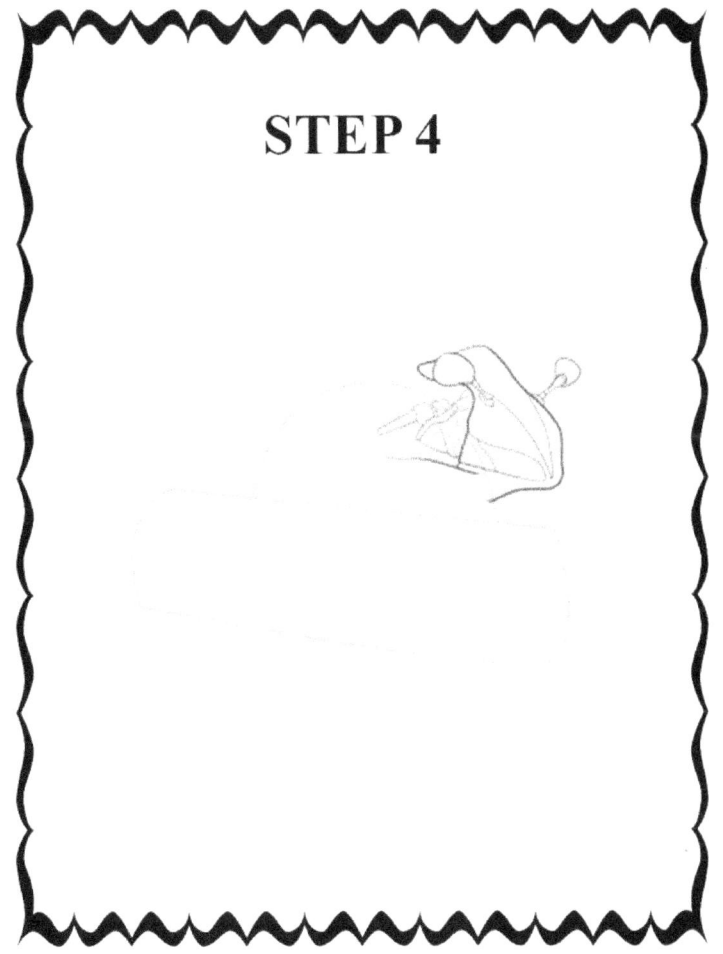

STEP 5

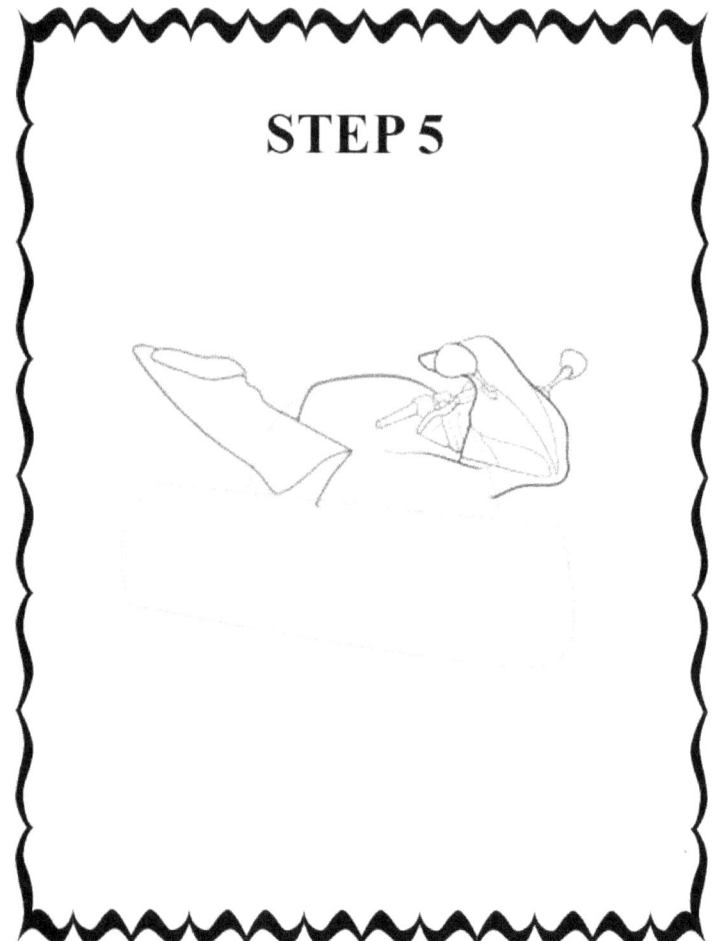

STEP 6

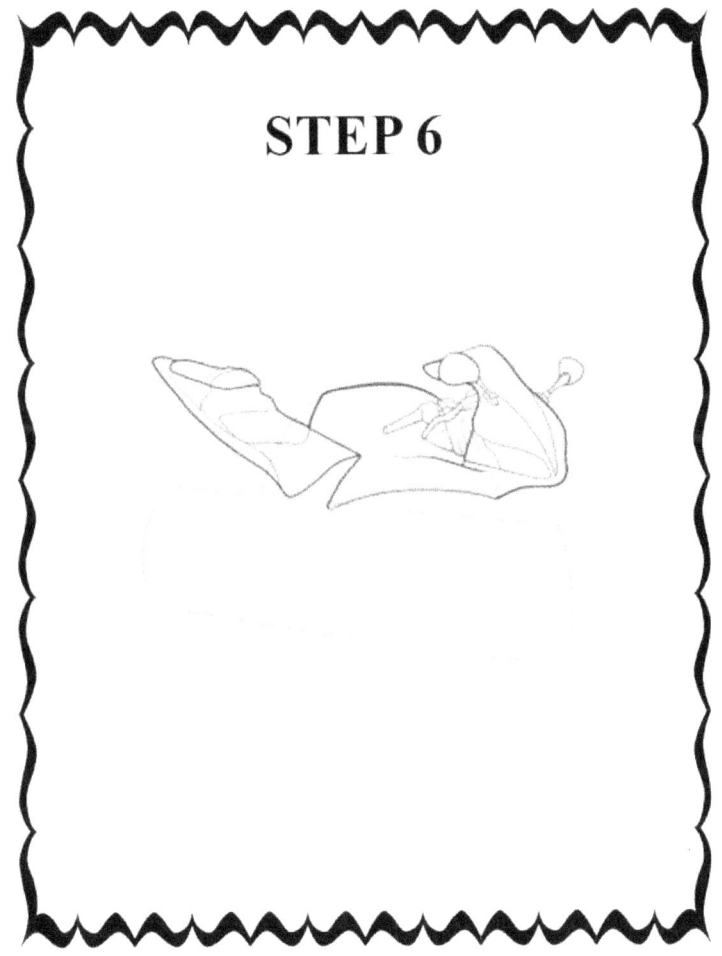

STEP 7

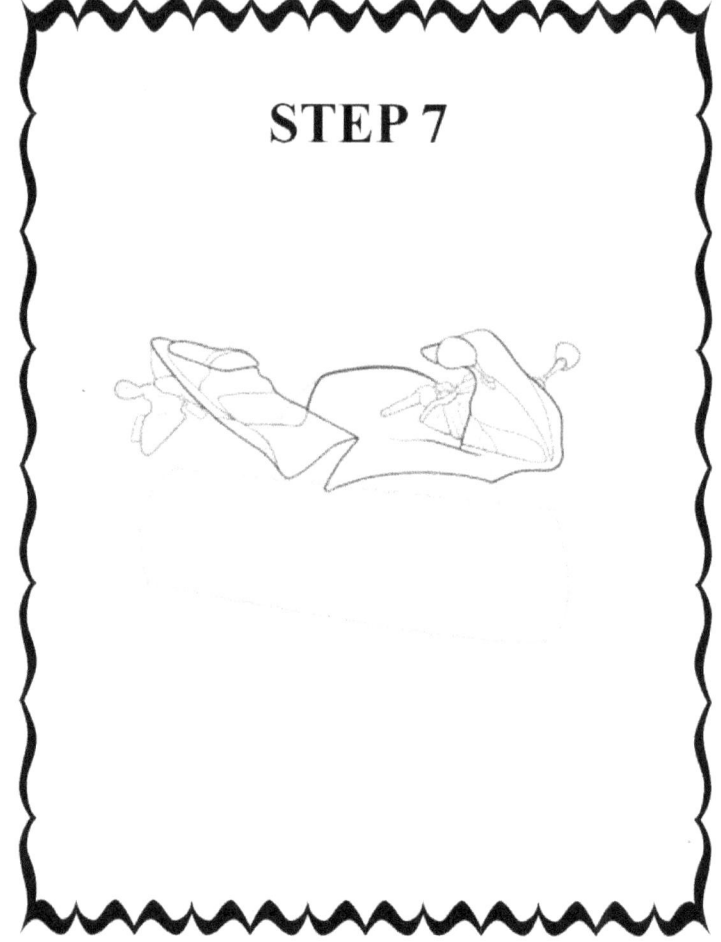

STEP 8

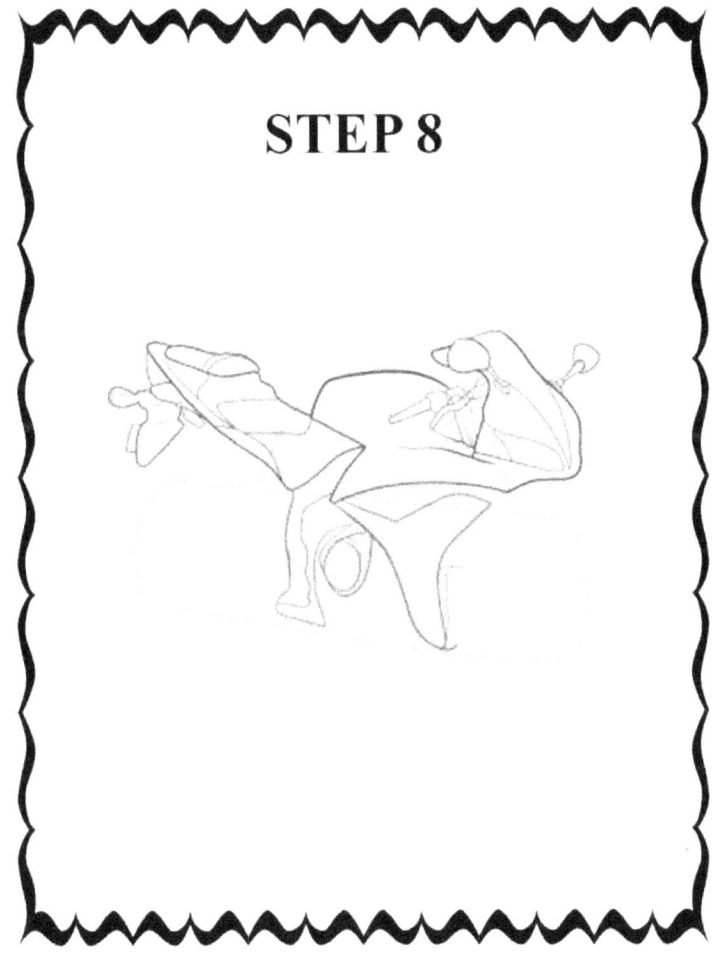

STEP 9

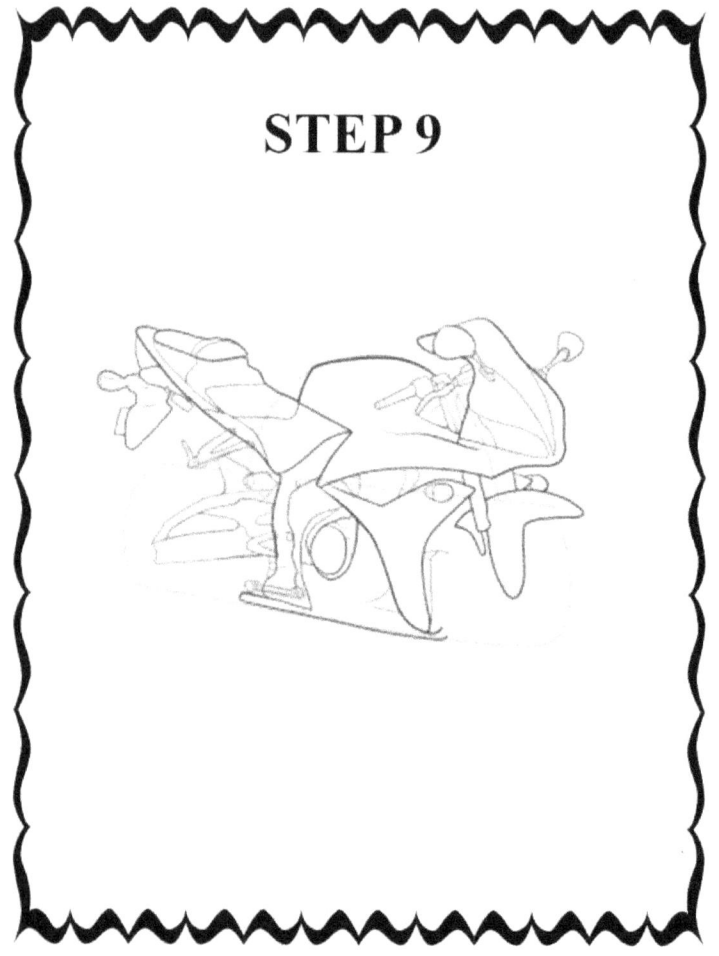

47

STEP 10

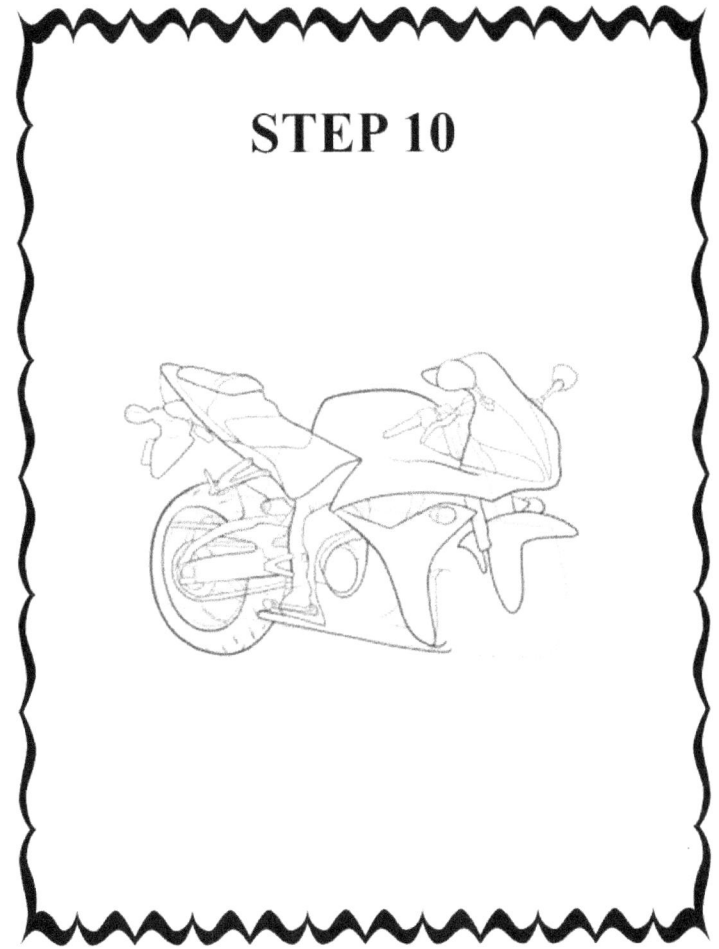

STEP 11

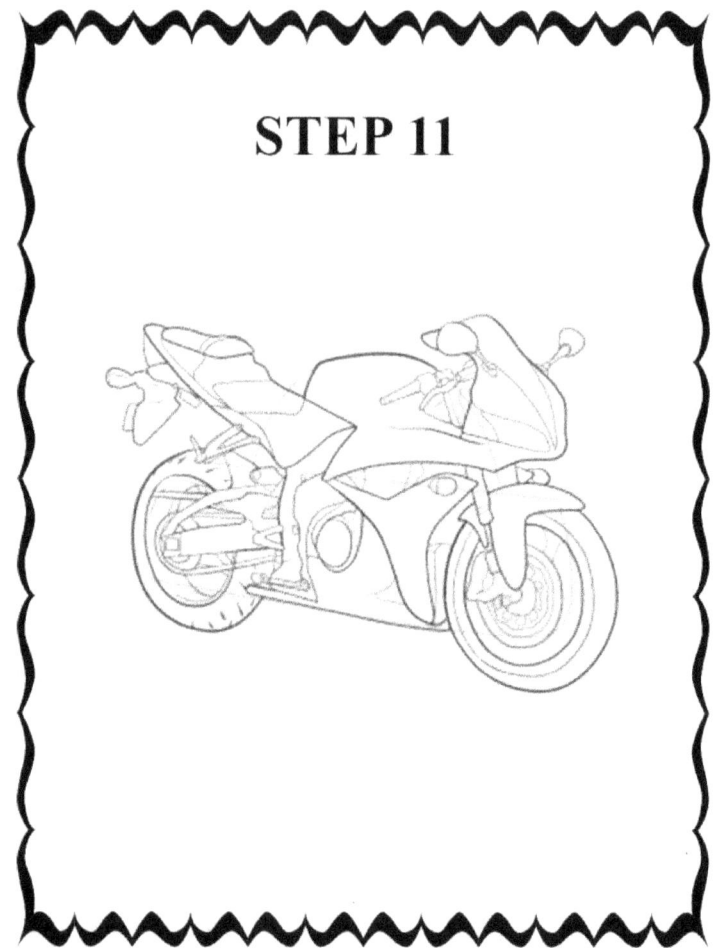

STEP 12

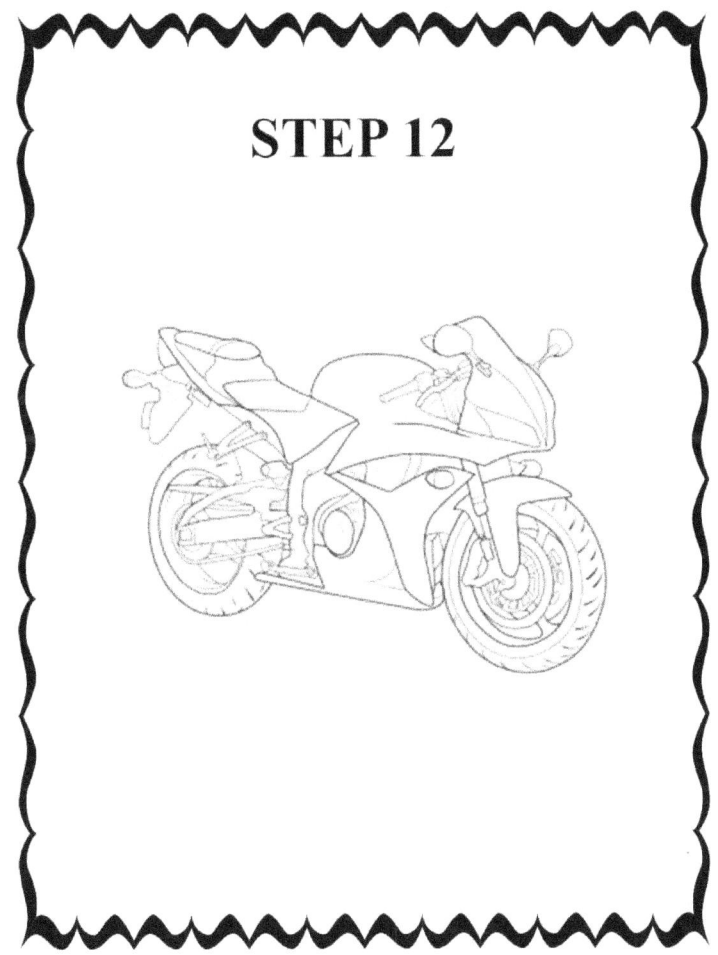

MOTORCYCLE

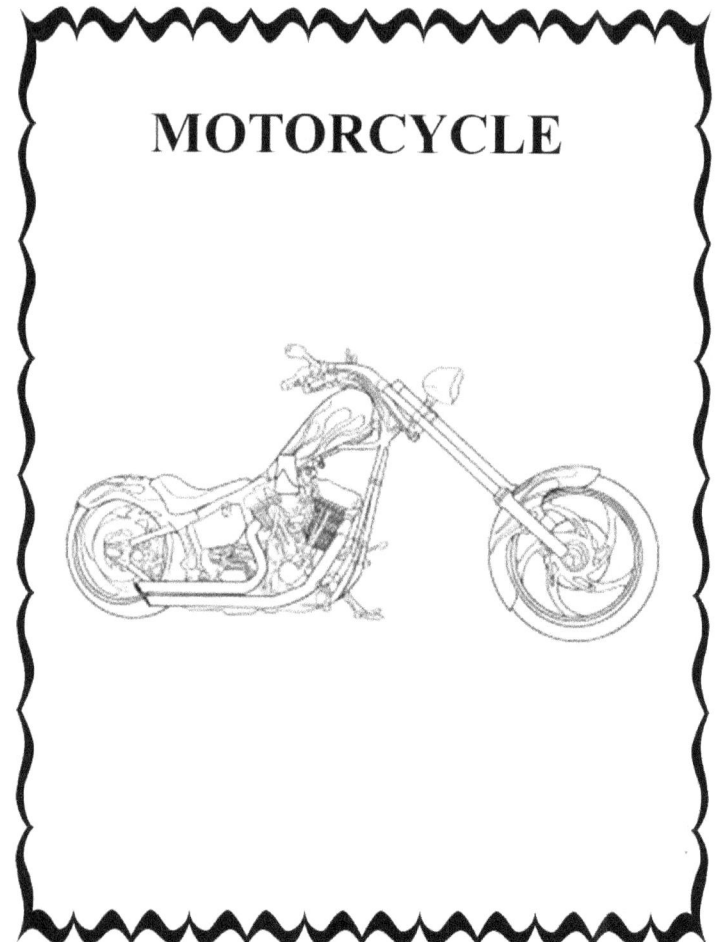

STEP 1

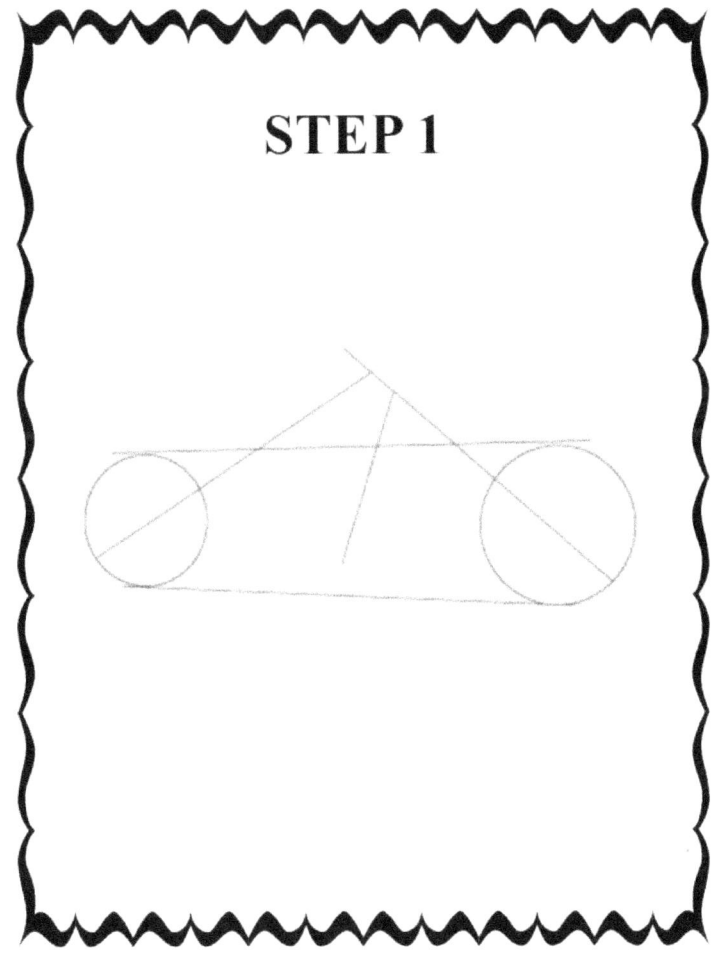

STEP 2

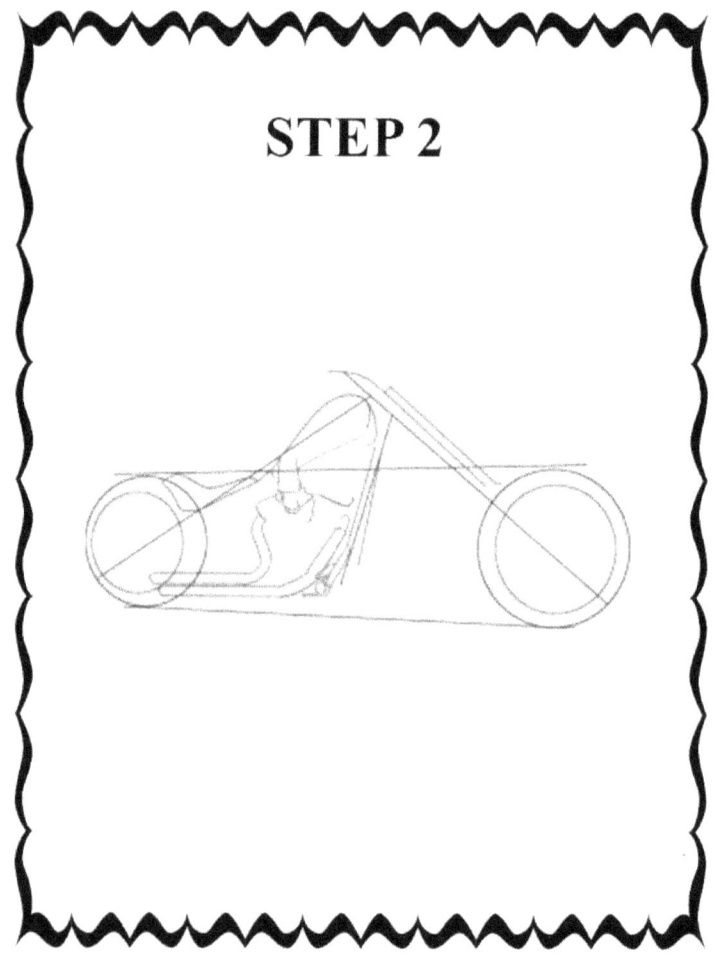

STEP 3

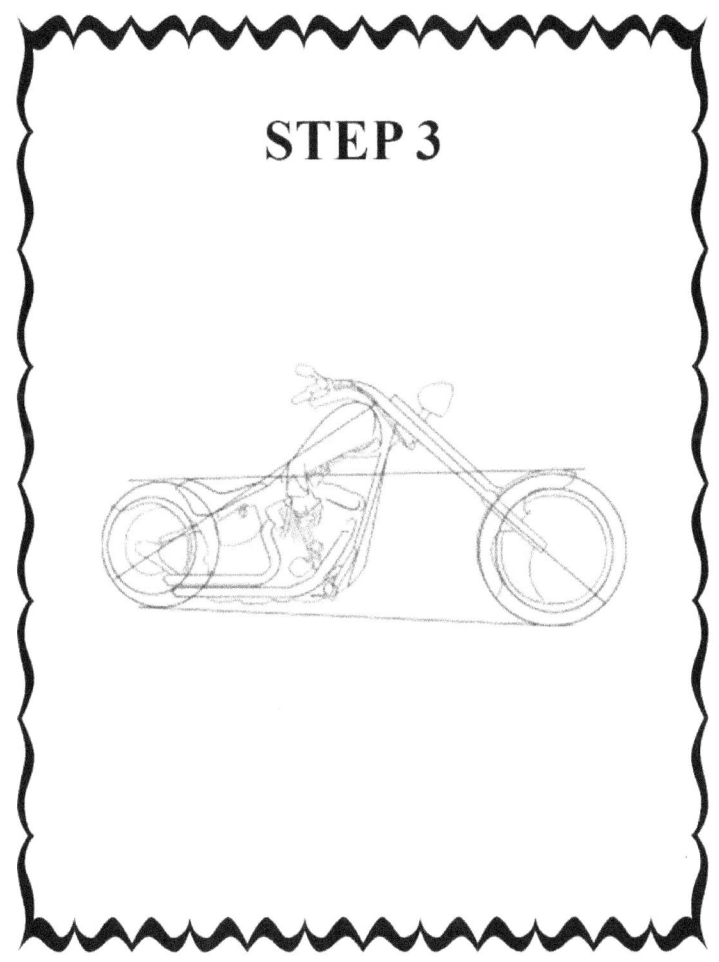

STEP 4

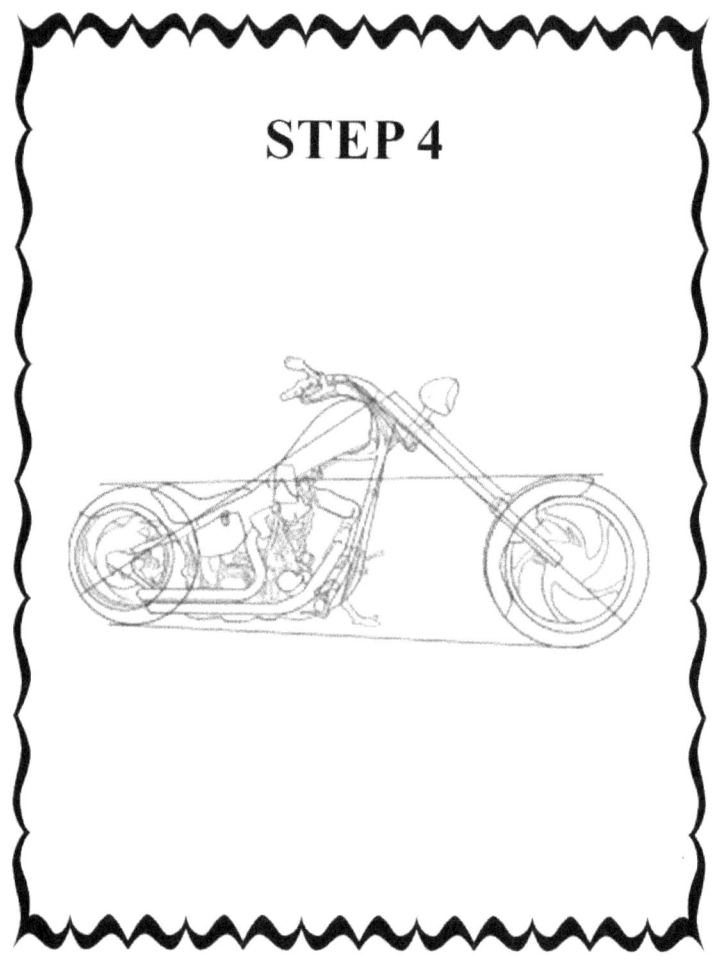

STEP 5

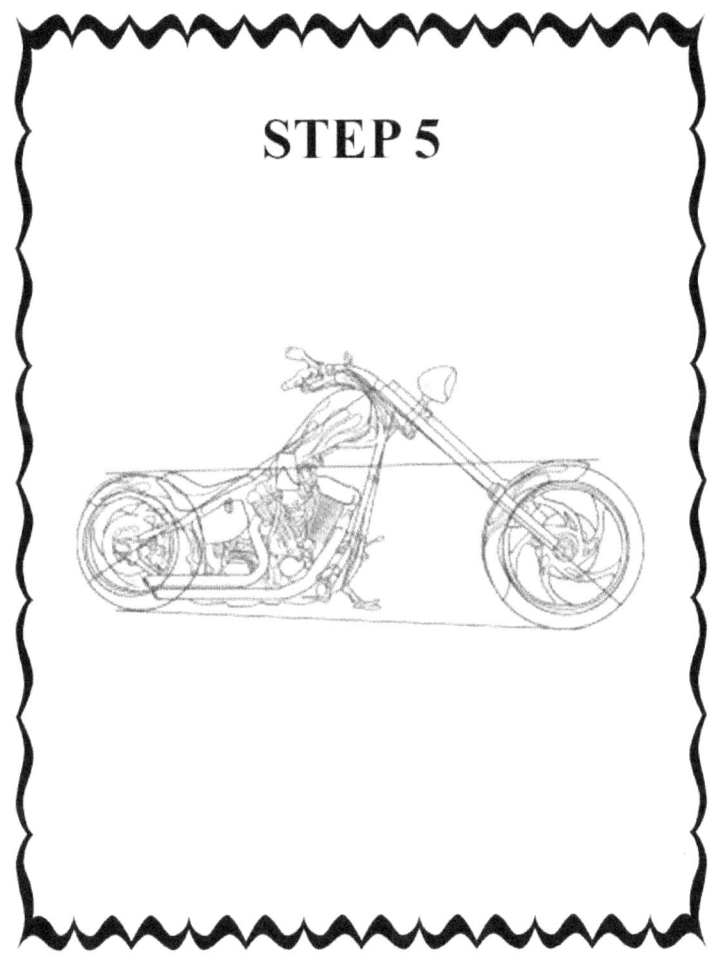

STEP 6

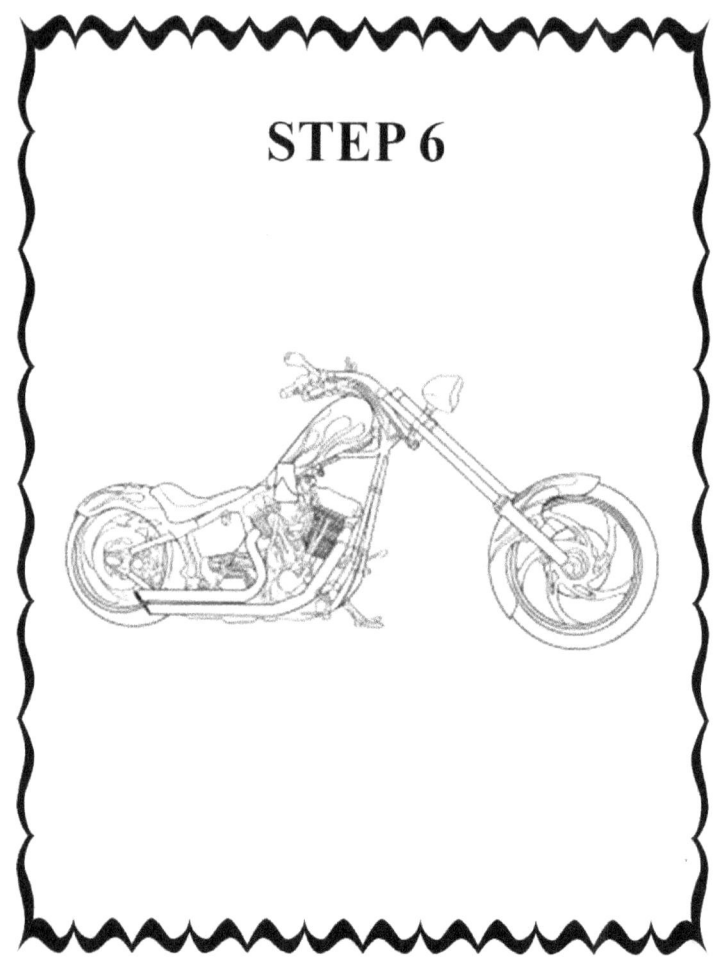

www.ingramcontent.com/pod-product-compliance
Lightning Source LLC
Chambersburg PA
CBHW071640170526
45166CB00003B/1367